Edward Roper

A Claim on Klondyke

A Romance

Edward Roper

A Claim on Klondyke
A Romance

ISBN/EAN: 9783744674027

Printed in Europe, USA, Canada, Australia, Japan

Cover: Foto ©Thomas Meinert / pixelio.de

More available books at **www.hansebooks.com**

ALONE IN THE VAST SOLITUDE.

A CLAIM ON KLONDYKE

A Romance

OF

THE ARCTIC EL DORADO

BY

EDWARD ROPER, F.R.G.S.

AUTHOR OF
'BY TRACK AND TRAIL THROUGH CANADA,' ETC., ETC.

WITH ILLUSTRATIONS

ILLUSTRATIONS.

	PAGE
ALONE IN THE VAST SOLITUDE	*Frontispiece*
SHOOTING MYLES CAÑON	44
LAKE LA BARGE	54
FIVE FINGERS RAPIDS	57
ON THE YUKON AT THE MOUTH OF THE KLONDYKE RIVER	61
OUR DUG-OUT, OUR TUNNEL, AND OUR SLUICE	76
"WHEN SHE APPEARED AGAIN I WAS GREATLY EMBARRASSED"	147
MAY AND I IN THE DUG-OUT	218
"IT WAS A MELANCHOLY UNDERTAKING"	224
"WELCOME, FRIENDS"	240

A CLAIM ON KLONDYKE.

PREAMBLE.

SOMEWHERE near midnight in January 1897, a man — important to this little history — stood on an expanse of glittering snow, amidst low forest-covered hills and rugged mountains which were draped in the same white garb. He was looking eagerly towards the north-west, and was listening intently.

This man was muffled to the eyes in furs, he wore a rough bearskin coat, and his head was enveloped in a huge capote. He wore snow-shoes, and a gun lay across his arm.

A grand long-haired dog was by his side; he was listening, seemingly as intently as his master.

The moon was shining full, the deep purple sky was sown thick with brilliant stars,—one could have read small print easily, it was so light.

Not a breath of air was stirring.

The intensity of the cold was indescribable: if

there had been the slightest wind, this man could not have stood thus, in this open space, and lived.

He was a large man really, but the immensity of his surroundings, the vast field of dazzling snow on which he stood, made him appear to be a pigmy, whilst his loneliness and solitude gave a note of unutterable melancholy to the scene.

Several minutes passed, neither dog nor man moving from this attitude of strained attention. All nature was absolutely motionless; no branch stirred in the near forest, nor was one flake of snow wafted by the softest zephyr — yet there was no silence. The far-off woods resounded with frequent sharp reports, as if firearms were being discharged there, the nearer rocks and trees from time to time gave forth detonations like fusilades of musketry, and beneath his feet—he stood on a broad space of water, turned to ice of unknown depth, cushioned deep with snow—were groanings, grindings, cracklings, and explosions. It was the terrible arctic cold that caused this tumult. One could almost fancy that these two figures, silhouetted black against the dazzling white, were frozen solid too.

At length the man moved, and, patting his companion's head with his gauntleted hand, spoke, "No, good dog," he sighed, "it's another hallucination." And the dog looked up at him, and whimpered, then turned his gaze again in the direction it had been before, with eagerness.

It was impossible to guess from this man's appearance what he was like: he was so enveloped in wrappers only his eyes were visible; but his voice proclaimed him to be gently bred—it had the accent of a cultivated Englishman.

"No good," he went on muttering. "Let us get back, old Patch, my sole companion in this awful wilderness; it was not a shot we heard, only the frost that made that clamour," and he made as if to move away.

But the dog evidently was not satisfied. He sat down, kept his nose pointed in the one direction, and whimpered again and again. The man stood still and listened.

"Strange, strange," he spoke aloud, "that Patch is so persistent; perhaps it will be well to go on a bit more. There's nothing to prevent it—no one waiting for us. I suppose it is about midnight by the moon; but night or day, it's pretty much the same up here. Yes; we'll go on along this frozen creek: one cannot well miss the way back."

He was silent for a few moments, then resumed, "I'm talking aloud to myself again! or is it to the dog? This isolation, this loneliness, is terrible; but, come, my lad, come on!" and he started.

Patch, seeing his master move, began to wag his bushy tail, and dance with delight; he flew ahead, barking and capering, but every now and then stopped suddenly, pricked up his sharp ears, and listened as his master did.

They must have pushed on a mile or more from where we first encountered them. The expanse of level snow had widened greatly. There were no trees near, the sound of the frost in rock and timber was distant and subdued, and they stood side by side again attentive.

Suddenly, away off in the ranges to their right, two reports were audible—unmistakably they were shots fired from a gun—and then immediately six sharp cracks resounded; it was the discharge of a revolver!

At the first noise, again the man's mittened hand sought the dog's collar to restrain him, for he was intensely excited. The moment the sixth revolver shot had sounded, he removed his hand, and shouted, " Forward, good dog; go sic 'em!" and the two rushed off in the direction of the sounds.

Another mile they covered rapidly, the dog running ahead and barking; then returning, looking eagerly and joyfully into his master's face, then hurrying on again.

But soon calling Patch to him, he held him and waited, hoping to hear more signs of human presence in that awful region. He was not disappointed.

Again two rapid gun shots were fired, and six revolver shots, and they were nearer than they had been before.

"Patch," said the man then, "we'll try what this will do," and lifting up his gun, he pulled one trigger, and a few seconds after the other. Then taking a revolver from his belt, he fired six cartridges slowly in the air.

What would come of this? would there be any response? He had not long to wonder. The signal was repeated, and he knew that there were fellow-creatures in those mountains. White, black, or red, he did not care then. The feeling that he was not alone in that white world, that terribly hard, frozen world, was enough for him.

He and the dog hurried on, ascended the low bare hill upon their right, and when after a vigorous climb they reached the summit, he fired again, as he had done before. Patch barked loudly, joyfully, and there came into his master's mind the certainty that he was on the point of some discovery, some adventure to break the monotony of his life.

The response was immediate. Down in the valley at his feet, but at some distance, what appeared to be a door was opened suddenly, revealing a light within, and in the illuminated space a figure stood, who, lifting up a gun, fired again. Next this figure ran out of the building brandishing a blazing pine-knot, and across the wide valley he distinctly heard the cry of a fellow-being, and, still more wonderful, more amazing, it sounded to be the voice of a woman in distress.

"Go to her, Patch!" he cried. The good dog obeyed, whilst he followed as rapidly as he could. It was rough ground, all rocks and fallen trees: he was exhausted ere he had traversed half the distance. Halting a moment to recover breath, he had a view against the bright light of the doorway of Patch crouched at the feet of the person there, who was stooping to caress him.

A few hundred yards more and he halted again for breath, and then he heard a long-drawn cry of agony. "Help, oh! help! whoever you are! Indian or white man, come, come and help!" And our friend called loudly across the waste: "I'm an Englishman! Trust me. I'm making my way to you with all the haste I can!" and over the snow-clad expanse resounded the response, "Thank God! thank God!"

CHAPTER I.

DURING the winter of 1895-96, I was staying at Bella Rocca, a boarding-house in Victoria, Vancouver Island, British Columbia. I had come to that charming city, on that beautiful island, to discover, if possible, an opening for the investment of my modest capital in a manner which would give me a more congenial way of making a livelihood than I had found in Eastern Canada, where I had resided for some few years.

When I first arrived in the Dominion, I settled in the backwoods of Ontario. Later, I had passed some years on the prairies, and later still, I had spent some time in the Rocky Mountains, the Selkirks, and on the Fraser river.

I had led a life of toil, I was well up in bush work and ways, but I did not like the life; so, having saved a little money, and having heard so much of the Pacific coast, I came to Victoria, as I have said.

At Bella Rocca a man was staying with whom I

became very friendly: he was an Englishman, about my age, and had many tastes congenial to me. He was idle, appeared to have plenty of money, and seemingly had no wish to do any work or business.

He was my frequent companion in my walks around Victoria: there being few idle people there, and I having much time unoccupied, this friendship was mutually agreeable.

I was puzzled for a while about him. He was very reticent about himself—I could not even tell if he had been long in Canada, although occasionally a few words fell from him which made me believe he knew it well.

It was towards March; I had found nothing to suit me; I had often told this friend what I was looking for, and had been quite open about my past, my present desires, and my experience in the country, when one day, as he and I were sitting on Beacon Hill, enjoying the soft spring weather, gazing with delight at the glorious Olympic range across the Straits of San Juan de Fuca, "Ah!" said my companion—his name was Percy Meade—"ah! it's not long now before I'll be outside there," and he pointed north to Cape Flattery and the Pacific Ocean.

"You are going across, then—to China or Australia?" I asked.

"Neither," replied he, with a smile; "I am going north by the first ship that sails."

"North!" I remarked. I was not greatly interested. "Well, I've never had the wish to go up the coast. What is to be done up there?"

He did not reply at once; but after a bit said he, "I wonder you have never tried gold-mining in this country; don't you think it's worth considering?"

I replied that I had heard so much about it in the mountains, and had read about the old days on the Fraser and the Cariboo, that I believed it to be a poor business, and supposed that every ounce of gold found cost two in labour and expense, and said many things that most men do who have not taken the gold-fever.

Meade said little more that day, but shortly after he asked me what I would do if I were told of a spot, by some one I could trust, where gold existed in large quantities, where any one who had the courage to go could pick it up, or at any rate obtain it, with comparatively little labour.

I replied that, no doubt, if such a chance were offered me I should accept it,—that I was as keen to make a pile as any one. "Only," I added, laughing, "I doubt if there are such places left, and still more that if any person knew of one he would tell me."

Meade was silent for some time, then, "Look here," he said, very seriously, "we've been together a few months; I can see the sort of fellow you are; you know what rough life is, I'm sure you can stand it better than most; so now, listen — I know of such a place, and I'll tell you about it on condition, naturally, that you'll keep it to yourself."

I smiled. "How do you know?" I asked, "and why do you tell me?"

To this he answered slowly and earnestly, "I was up north all last season — on the Yukon. I found a place on our side that is full of gold; you would hardly believe it if you saw it, but it is so. It is on a creek up a river that joins the Yukon in British territory, about seventy-five miles from the boundary, not far from the ruins of Fort Reliance.

"I went from Seattle last spring up the coast round the Alaskan peninsula, into Behring Sea, and so to Fort St Michael, where I landed. Then I proceeded up the Yukon in a stern-wheel steamer to a place they call Fort Cudahy, or the Forty Mile, in British territory. It was a terribly long journey — four thousand three hundred and fifty miles from here. It took eight weeks, and cost a big sum. There was a little mining going on up the river, but different from any I had seen, and I have been to Australia. I did not like the look of it. The diggers were scattered about, getting what they called flour-gold, and not so very much of that.

"The season during which washing can be done is very short — four months at most; but then it is broad daylight always, no night at all; men work ceaselessly — ay, and women too.

"I tried a little here and there, I 'prospected' about, and in time I got up the big river some long way indeed, until I came to a collection of shacks and shanties, with a store or two, that they call Dawson City. I was short of everything then but money, of which I still had a moderate supply; so I obtained some stores and a decent outfit, and after a few days of misery in the wretched place, I loaded all into a canoe which I bought, and pushed on, quite alone, up a river which joined the Yukon there. It was the THRON-DUICK — the Klondyke as it is called now. Paddling slowly up this stream, I landed frequently, seldom finding gold, and I always tried the soil as I went along. Occasionally I found the colour, once or twice enough to pay, I fancied, with good machinery. There was a fascination about this life. I believed that any moment some pan of gravel that I washed might be rich and give me all I wanted—a golden claim.

"I kept on thus until I must have been at least forty miles up this river. I passed several branches, for to me the main stream looked most promising, until I came to one, much narrower: it joined in with a rush and roar, and I liked the look of it. I landed, walked up it, and liked it so that I determined to ascend it if possible. I could not get my laden canoe up the steep water—I must therefore 'portage.' I set to work; I carried my stuff past the rapid. It was a tough job getting my canoe up, but by good luck I did. Then I went on again, trying here and there as usual.

"When I was too tired to keep on, I put up my little tent ashore and slept. When rested, on I went again.

"I had quite lost reckoning; I had no idea of the day of the week or month, but the sun indicated that the summer was going. It would not do to be caught up there as unprovided as I was. I thought I had come far enough, so, reluctantly, I made up my mind that I would after another day or two retrace my steps.

"That very day I found what I had looked for. I hit upon a bar on this creek, where gold was so thick that I was bewildered.

"I suppose you know how gold is washed? Well, I had no need to wash—I picked out of that heap of gravel in three days over seventy-five pounds' weight of it!"

"Seventy-five pounds of gold! Why, that was worth £3000!" I cried.

"Yes, quite that," said Meade; "but I got £2500 for it here, and have a decent little bag of nuggets still unsold. I'll show them to you at the bank some day if you like."

I smiled. I'm afraid I did not altogether believe him. I had an idea that he was romancing. "How did you get down and bring all that gold with you?" I asked, half laughing.

"It's too long a yarn to tell now," he replied. "I got back all right to Dawson in my canoe, sold it, and managed to keep my find secret. I fortunately procured a passage in the stern-wheeler, P. B. Weare, the last boat for St Michael's that season. From there I easily got here, and no one knew that I had struck gold—no one does know it yet but the manager of the bank, and now you."

It was a most interesting story, certainly; I was glad to have heard it, but there was "no such luck for me," I observed, at which Meade laughed, but added, "See here, I've told you this because I want you to share with me this season! What d'ye say?"

"What?" I exclaimed, "and get gold like that? Oh! of course I'll go; but are you in earnest? why should you favour me thus?"

He declared solemnly that he meant it; he averred that he had taken to me, that he knew I was strong, healthy, a good fellow, and used to working in rough country, and as he was determined to go, and certainly would not do so again alone, he had made me his confidant and this offer in perfect good faith, and he ended thus, "Think it over, take time, keep what I've told you to yourself, but I hope you'll join me."

Later, he explained that we must leave Victoria soon, that we should come back at the end of September, and that he would be miserably surprised if we did not return with reasonable piles. "But we will not go the way I went," said he. "No, I met some men at Dawson who had come by a much shorter route—by the Lynn Canal and Skagway. We save thus nearly 3000 miles, and the trail is quite feasible. You've done some boating, some canoeing, I suppose?"

I said I had, both in England and Canada, which pleased him, and he assured me that we should do splendidly, and again he said he hoped I'd join him.

Naturally, I did think this over. I heard about his antecedents from the bank manager, found he was a member of a good old English family, and that he himself was of good repute. I heard from the same source that it was true about the gold he had brought down, I saw his bag of nuggets, and I liked him. I was looking for some employment, I counted the cost, and knowing that if, at the worst, I returned empty-handed, I should not even then be quite without funds, I consented to share with him in the adventure. He was to defray all expenses.

It was early in April that he and I started in a steamer bound for Sitka and other ports in Alaska. She came from Tacoma, in the State of Washington, and picked us up at Victoria on her way to the north.

Meade having all plans cut and dried, it did not take us long to lay in our stock of necessaries. We purchased provisions, tinned meats and vegetables, flour and bacon, with plenty of various preserved foods, enough to keep us going well for at least a year. We took ample supply of tobacco, with guns, ammunition, a sheet-iron Yukon stove, picks, shovels, washpans, and we did not forget our axes. All these goods were done up in parcels covered with waterproof canvas, each in weight suitable for "packing," that is for Indians to carry.

Leaving Victoria, we travelled up between Vancouver Island and the mainland to Naniamo. Here we took in coal, then headed up the coast.

How am I to describe to you this wonderful journey? Words fail me. From the very start it was delightful. True, we were at sea; but being amongst islands, we were so sheltered that it was like a placid river. We traversed the grandest scenery that can be imagined, the water clear and smooth as glass, with air as soft as velvet. We sighted Queen Charlotte's Islands, but voyaged through channels nearer the mainland, between grand timbered islets, past rocky bluffs and gorges, always in sight of mountains, many being snow-covered and glaciered. Then on between Prince of Wales' Island and the mainland, and so to Fort Wrangel, where we left the goodly steamer. We had come seven hundred miles in her, and had been four days on the way.

Wrangel was just a rough group of shanties, with some stores and many totem-poles, as most of the few inhabitants were Indians of the Stickeen tribe.

The whites were traders, or miners and prospectors, *en route* to the Yukon country. Here we hired a canoe to carry us to Juneau. It was an immense one, beautifully fashioned out of one huge log of cedar—a dug-out—but in shape and seaworthiness most excellent. We engaged four Indians to man it. Most of the trip was made with paddles; but sometimes a square sail was hoisted on a pole forward. We camped each night upon the rocky shores.

It took three days to reach that town. It is the metropolis of Alaska, Sitka being the capital. But most of the business is done in Juneau. It is, naturally, a rough and ramshackle place, yet we found it possible to obtain fair accommodation at a queer hotel, and every article of provisions and gear needed in the upper country. It has a city hall and court-house, waterworks, banks, and electric light and wharves! We had to wait two days for one of the two small steamers which ply between Juneau and Skagway. The Rustler is the one we took, the fare then being only 10 dollars each—but we had to feed ourselves.

After leaving Juneau we steamed along a narrow strait between Douglas Island and the coast, and entered the famed Lynn Canal, which is an arm of the sea running almost due north. It averages ten miles in width, and is about one hundred in length, having very regular shores, straight and uniform; but for its dimensions, it might be taken indeed for an artificially made canal. On our **left we skirted** the great **Davidson** Glacier. **The** whole journey was **grand,** sublime, and in many places awful.

We arrived in Skagway Inlet on the second day. **A few** miles from the head of **it we** came to **the** Skagway river or creek, 120 miles from Juneau, and here, amongst a wilderness of trees, **mountains, and** mud flats, a mere **foothold** in the snow-clad granite coast-range, were a handful **of Indian rancheries and** a few log shanties and some tents. There is a great rise and fall **in the tides** at **Skagway. We** had to wait some time ere the one boat belonging to the Rustler **could land** us and our stuff on **the** rock-strewn muddy **beach.** No one from the shore lent a **hand.** There **was** a rough wharf, it is true, in course **of** construction. The men building it, we understood, had gone to **their** camp, for it was late when we arrived.

A number **of** Indians were about : their sole employment **seemed to** be to sit on stumps and logs, smoke and chew **tobacco,** and gaze stolidly at **us.** They **were** dressed **just** like the white men.

As for the few white **men,** they gathered round **us,** eyed us and our outfit, **but** said nothing. **A more** miserable, unhappy, low-spirited set of men I had **never** before come across.

Well, we were landed at Skagway, and questioned **the inhabitants.** It was not easy to obtain information. " **Where** is the trail to the White Pass ? How could **we** get to **it** ? What means of transport were

B

there ?" Those were the questions we made it plain that we desired to have answered.

One would have supposed that these people could have enlightened us; but no — their advice and information was so vague that we might have taken them for new arrivals, like ourselves. But that they were old hands was plain, for they argued amongst themselves, entered into long yarns about what this and that man had experienced, what Slim Jim thought, and Blear-eyed Scottie said — we could make nothing of them. Some advised us to go by canoe, which was chaff; and others declared that was ridiculous — by the trail was the only way. "What trail? Which is it?" we begged to be informed. "Oh! just up the river a piece," was all we could arrive at.

No doubt these men, regarding us as "tenderfeet," took pleasure, as usual, in mystifying us; and it was our policy not to undeceive them. I was the usual spokesman.

It must be quite clearly understood that the rush to the Klondyke had not begun then. It was known, undoubtedly, that there was much gold up country, and every white man there was after it, so that if it had been guessed that Meade had been up already, the fact of his returning with the ample outfit we possessed would have convinced them that he had been successful, and we should have been followed and our secret discovered.

It was ten o'clock at night then, but not really

dark. We were perplexed. These loafers gradually dispersed, and only one man hung behind, who had been silent hitherto. When we were alone with him he became communicative. We knew, directly he spoke, that he was an Englishman of a better sort, and he recognised what we were.

Said he, "Let me advise you: get all your stuff piled up yonder; put up your tent and turn in; in the morning you'll find all easy. There's a man here who bosses everything — white folks and Indians; he's a Yankee, true enough, but a decent fellow; he keeps a sort of a boarding-house, and has a store; he's a fur-buyer, a trader, and a packer; he'll straighten things out for you."

Accordingly, in the morning, after we had fed, Indians and loafers gathered around again, and for a bit it looked as if the difficulty would continue; but shortly our English friend, who was working at the wharf building, and whose sobriquet, we found, was "Colney Hatch," usually shortened to "Coney" (he explained that he foolishly one day let it be known that that famous institution was near his home in England), well, this man came to us, and took us with him to Boss Parkinson's — the man he had mentioned.

We found the boss was certainly a "live" man: in five minutes he had cleared all up. He shook hands heartily, asked us if we had any money, where we proposed to go, with a few other questions.

Having satisfied him on these points, "Come on," said he; "guess we will soon fix things. Thar's but one way from here to Dawson City. You've got to have your gear packed to the Windy Arm, that's sure. It'll cost you 14 dollars for every hundred pounds. How much you got?"

We took him to our pile. He was surprised. "Land sakes!" he exclaimed. "Why, what'n tarnation! There ain't bin one party through yere yet fixed like you fellers; 'n say—guess you bin through before. No; wall some person's told you who has been—eh?"

We admitted we had had good advice. "Wall, so I jedge," he went on. "Why, darn me, if you hain't got every pack just right!" and he lifted one or two. "50 lb. each, I reck'n?"

We said that was so, and that each man could carry two; and as we had exactly 800 lb. of grub, and about 200 lb. weight of tent, blankets, and cooking gear and tools, we considered it would take just about twelve Indians to do what was required comfortably.

"Gee-rusalem!" cried our new acquaintance; "'n you're fixed to pay 140 dollars for this yere job?"

"Oh yes, we can," I replied; "but it seems these Indians around are idle—can't it be done for less?"

"Idle!—Great Scot!" he yelled with laughter. "Why, stranger, they're a restin'—you bet they need it. Hold on till you see the kind o' journey they've got to make—lor! and you too—you stop till you've felt fifty, 'n mebbe a hundred pounds o' pack on your backs, 'n then I guess you'll think them 140 dollars ain't so easy airned. These yere Si-washes ain't like them red fellers of the plains—nossir. These work, they do; m—m—I guess so. You pay me that 140 dollars, 'n I guess all will go slick."

A few dollars one way or the other were no particular consequence to us, and we thought it wiser to keep dark, so we agreed; at which the boss, calling to an Indian, took him aside.

Ten minutes after there was excitement in the camp. From listless, silent logs, the whole tribe woke up, and from that moment showed of what stuff they were made. We learnt from the boss what our route would be after reaching Lake Tagish. He told us about Miles Cañon and the White Horse Rapids, which he assured us were the only real difficulties we had to face. He advised us to hire an Indian to go with us who knew the way to the foot of the White Horse, anyway.

The Stick (Stickeen) Indians are an avaricious people, they are shrewd and tricky, a good match for whites at bargains, and will do anything for money, which they know the value of right well. They are fine strapping fellows, and are proud to tell you they are "aller same King George man"—*i.e.*, Englishmen; but I believe they say to Yankees that they are "aller same Boston man," which means Americans. They are evidently pretty deep, have a great love for tobacco and all intoxicants, and every beverage that possesses a " tang." They are supposed to be diminishing in numbers rapidly—there were thought to be only about one thousand left of them then.

It was sixty-five miles from Skagway to the Windy Arm of Lake Tagish, we were told, and that if we averaged ten miles a-day we should do well.

Within an hour our march began—that is, our Indians loaded four canoes with our packs; then we paddled six miles up-stream, landed, and camped for the night.

Our men were cheery; some spoke the Chinook jargon,—" the trade language of the Pacific coast,"—a few knew a little English. One who appeared to be their head man knew most, and he attached himself closely to us, cooked and helped us. It was our policy to appear " green," and this man, believing it was our first night in the bush, showed us how to manage. He called himself Jim Crow; this name had been given him by some facetious countryman of ours.

Starting at six the following morning, we soon understood what packing over the White Pass meant. There was a trail, sure enough; it consisted of a path winding through thick forest, up steep and rocky hills, some of them almost perpendicular; across swift running brooks, and beds of spongy moss—up to one's waist in places. There were clumps of coarse grass, thickets of brambles and the terrible devil's club thorn; so, before we had gone a couple of miles, we were satisfied that every cent we paid these Indian packers was well " airned " indeed.

For ourselves, it was all we could do to get on, carrying only our guns, and a small shoulder-bag with a little grub; whilst our boys plodded on, grunting but cheery, with their one hundred pounds apiece.

As we ascended gradually, we realised that it was becoming colder. We had not done three miles by noon when we came to snow. Jim Crow —Jim is what we called him of course—ordered a halt, and said they were well pleased,—that it was probably snow in the pass; some of them would go ahead without burdens and investigate —if so, they would return for sledges, "sleds"; they were very happy at this prospect. Accordingly two men went on. We rested, boiled some tea, and ate. In a couple of hours they returned, and had a pow-wow, resulting in some of them starting back to Skagway, whilst our tent was erected, a huge camp-fire built, and we prepared to pass the night, as Jim told us it would be too late when they returned with sleds to push on. We were somewhat annoyed at what we thought delay, but he assured us this plan would shorten the journey greatly.

It was midnight when they returned. They brought five sleds. On these, next day — which was hot and the snow was melting—all our goods were lashed, and that evening, when the crust upon the snow was frozen, we were off.

Our route lay up a shelving mountain-side overlooking a deep cañon. Snow-capped ranges and many small glaciers were constantly in sight across the valley, and every depression, on our side, held a trickling rivulet, a roaring stream, or more frequently a morass, knee-deep in moss and sodden grasses. The snow was not deep, but it was soft and slushy — the travelling was terrible, yet in spite of all we made what Jim called "good time."

It was noon next day ere we reached the timber line, and all above this was open and rocky. The snow was heavier here; in the shade it was frozen solid; the sleds travelled over it easily. Meade and I had all we could do to keep up with them; indeed we had let them get some distance ahead at one time, and when we caught them they were camped beside a great rock with stunted trees about it, and Jim said that we were very near the summit.

We camped that night in considerable comfort,— it was dry and cold, but having good blankets and plenty of fuel, Meade and I were cosy enough. Our Indians made shelters of sticks and brushwood and thin blankets, and built a huge fire. They played "poker"; their "chips" were beans.

An immense amount of snow falls on these coast

ranges; luckily we had none during our crossing—neither did it rain, which was wonderful.

Now, as to this White Pass ever being made the highway to the Yukon, I must say a few words. The trail as it then existed was absolutely impracticable for horses—it was all that men could do to clamber up it, and we realised that with much traffic, even of human beings, it would quickly become impassable, and yet Meade and I felt confident that with comparatively little work and some engineering skill a road, and some day even a railroad, could be made across it. Most of the runs of water could be bridged easily, in the rough way which is the custom in the wilds. Many of the morasses, we could see, could be drained by a few gutters cut with a spade. There being such a slope it was easy to run water off, and where that was impossible log causeways—corduroys—could be built with no great trouble, for logs were plentiful for the cutting. It was possible to wind round most of the rocks, and a few pounds of dynamite or giant powder would quickly clear the impassable masses. Certainly when we crossed it was terrible enough; but yet we plainly saw that a good road, fairly easy to traverse by horses, even with loaded waggons, was certain ere long to exist there.

If it should be proved that gold was plentiful in the Yukon country,—" Undoubtedly," we said, "before two years are past there will be a fine road here," and as to the gold—well, we had reason to be very sure about that.

From this camp the trail led up a narrow and precipitous defile until the actual summit was reached. We were then at least fifteen miles from Skagway, and near three thousand feet above tide-water.

From here there was a sheer descent of many feet to a lake—Summit Lake. It was frozen solid. The Indians assured us it was always frozen—that the snow never left its margin. At one point the ice overlapped the edge, forming a small glacier. A few yards below it was thawing. At some far distant day a great glacier had been there, for a cañon had been formed, and down it, beside the rushing stream of white water, our course lay. Mountains rose high around us, covered with ever-lasting snow.

Gradually the snow on our course disappeared and the sleds became useless, and Jim assured us that for the rest of the journey to Windy Arm packing must be resorted to. Therefore next morning the sleds were câched, and we started on our weary tramp.

Everything was frozen solid still, for it was not yet May. The travelling was exceedingly arduous,—not that there were any mountains to traverse or swamps to push through; it was simply a rough rock-strewn country, sparsely covered with scraggy trees, mostly pines and spruces, with bushes which we thought were willows, and long coarse grass.

We had five days of this, and then we reached the Windy Arm, and the Indians' contract was completed. We had come about sixty-five miles from Skagway.

It was still winter here: there was no open water, the woods were full of snow, which had been long since driven by strong winds from the open; it was a bleak and dreary outlook. Around the lake most of the timber had been fired, gaunt grey sticks alone were standing, and the ground was covered with half-burned logs and branches. Of fuel there was no lack. We made camp in the only close clump of living trees about. We put our tent up securely, made ourselves comfortable, for we knew we must stay on there and by some means build a boat or raft, and wait for the ice to break up. Thus our object was gained in reaching that spot, and we were ready to avail ourselves instantly of the open water, and to pursue our journey.

The Indians had behaved so exceedingly well that I proposed, and Meade agreed, to give them each a dollar.

Through Jim we signified our intention: he made them clearly understand that this was "potlach" —that is, a present. It gave great satisfaction, and when we added a plug of tobacco to each man, there was rejoicing in the camp.

We had taken quite a liking to Jim. He was seemingly proud to be more noticed by us than the others. He was an exceedingly handy fellow, and so far as we could make out from his very peculiar English and Chinook, he knew all about the route we had to follow, and was an experienced boatman. He had "shot" the Grand Cañon twice, and knew the way to get past the White Horse Rapids. He was apparently about five-and-twenty, a tall, athletic fellow, and with us very bright and talkative, although with his fellows he was taciturn. Like them he was keen after money, yet did not appear to realise that we were going up to where we hoped it would be plentiful. It is difficult to understand an Indian's apathy on this matter—along the Fraser, at Cariboo, and even in Alaska, they will work at washing gold, and seem quite satisfied to make a dollar or two a-day; but to undertake any plan for making a big lot at once they have no notion. It is perhaps because the idea of accumulating anything is not an Indian's nature.

Meade formed the idea that it would be well to induce this fellow to go with us to Lake La Barge. With this intent we plied him with information about gold, assuring him that, if he went with us, he would get plenty, so that he could return to the coast a rich man. This prospect had no charms for him, yet he liked the idea of the trip, and said that if we would pay him "ikt dolla la sun"—that is, in plain English, one dollar a-day—he would go; but when he added that he must bring his klootchman, his wife, with him, I was taken aback. Meade, however, was in favour of it—he considered it would be an additional inducement for Jim to stay, that she would probably be useful, and no trouble to us.

He questioned the fellow closely as to her age, her abilities; and he made us understand that she was young, could cook and paddle well, speak English, and would "mamook elan wash pil chickamin," which meant that she would help wash for gold. Her name, he announced, was Fanny; and Meade confided to me that he had a particular liking for that name, so we were induced to enter into the arrangement.

About "muck a muck"—*i.e.*, food—Jim said they would provide themselves; that he would go back to Skagway with the party and bring his wife out, and a load of all they needed, in six "la suns," six days. All that he stipulated for was that we should have nothing to do with Tagish Indians and that he should have "plenty 'bacca."

Of this we had a good supply; but thinking it would be no harm to have still more, we sent a little "chit" by him to Boss Parkinson, telling him how we had got on, and begging him to send out to us by Jim, if he discovered that they really meant to come with us, another dozen pounds of that fascinating weed.

The following day the band left us, and Meade and I were left alone in our glory.

CHAPTER II.

MEADE and I were by this time great friends: our tastes and aims were exactly alike—it was very nice. We had mutual acquaintances in England—we were the best of companions.

In our tent, with our sheet-iron stove going, our beds of thick layers of sweet-scented spruce twigs on rubber ground-sheets, with plenty of good blankets, we were quite cosy, and we had a few books with us.

Our surroundings were gloomy and uninteresting enough — just a dreary rock-strewn waste. Here and there were patches of faded grass, flattened by the snow which had covered it for months. A few gnarled and twisted cedars and spruces still grew about there; but gaunt, black-butted, dead pine-trees, their tops whitened by the frost and wind, were everywhere—the dry bones of the forest. The frozen lake and the coast range close behind us, the mountains to right, left, and ahead, were snow-covered and dismal, and there was no sign of life, no trace of a living creature.

It rained steadily for two days, and as it was freezing hard at the same time, everything was encased in ice. On the third day the clouds were scattered, and each twig and leaf and blade flashed and sparkled gloriously in the brilliant sun-rays. This only lasted a few hours, for the heat of the sun being great, this beautiful scene was soon spoiled. However, we hoped that a few such days would make havoc with the ice upon the lake, and we should have open water. But this was not to be just yet, for on the fourth day it blew hard from the east, and that night it snowed again and froze as hard as ever.

"On time," as Yankees say, Jim and his wife arrived: they came bounding along the trail, full of glee,—we thought them like children coming home from school. Jim was most voluble; a stream of the best English he knew, and jargon, fell unceasingly from his mouth. He was proud of his wife, that was clear—he showed her off, asking our opinion of her, giving us to understand that she was as good as she appeared.

I must say that she was well worth his praise, in looks at any rate; her other good qualities we discovered later.

She was unmistakably an Indian woman: her colour was warm brown, she had beautiful eyes, and a very amiable expression. Her hair was her pride: it was not straight and coarse—it waved, even curled some little, and glistened in the sun as if it were black spun glass.

We took to her at once: she appeared to be of a bright and happy disposition, and not an atom like our preconceived notions of a squaw. Meade subsequently made a sketch of her in her ordinary dress.

But what charmed us greatly was, she could speak English quite understandably, and when she informed us that she was "one Metlakahtla gal," and had been trained under the eye of good Mr Duncan, we felt we were fortunate to have her with us, and we never ceased to impress on Jim what a lucky dog he was. He seemed to think so himself—at least Fan said he did. They put up a little canvas tepee, or wigwam, near. They had brought it with them on their sled, with their entire household gear, which was not much. It consisted mostly of dried salmon which was to be their food. We added some of ours to it occasionally, and later when we killed game we shared it with them. Fan cooked for us, and we believed she religiously refrained from pilfering our food. She had certainly been well trained.

After this we had a few days clear, calm, and sunny. Pools of water formed on land amongst the rocks and tangle, and the lake-ice was awash, yet Jim assured us that we need not expect the lake to open yet, and Fan added, "By'me by we get plenty freeze once more, and, mebbe, plenty snow!"

C

In this latter she was mistaken: she was right about the freeze, though. Thick ice formed every night, if night it could be called. One day it blew a heavy gale: we kept under cover, wondering that our little tent was not carried bodily away.

The matter of a boat occupied our consideration. Jim had heard that two men, camped down on Tagish Lake, had a whip-saw, and were cutting lumber to sell to parties like us to build their boats with, but our only means of getting to them was by a raft. There was no timber fit for boat-building in our neighbourhood, therefore when weather permitted we chopped and rolled logs on to the ice, and lashed and pinned them together into a form we hoped would bear us safely. We built it on the ice so that when that broke up it would be afloat.

Jim and his wife helped: she was as active as a young deer, and as strong as either of us.

Two weeks passed thus. Our raft was finished, and we were waiting patiently for the ice to disappear. We had spells of very hot weather, plenty of wind, but very little rain. The sun did not set till late; by two A.M. it was up again. The growth of vegetation was amazing—grass was green, and flowers had sprung into bloom, seemingly in a few hours. A few birds were seen, robins and jays.

One evening a flock of ducks whistled over the tent. Meade sprang up, gun in hand, but too late for a shot; but next day more passed and we bagged several brace. It was evident that spring had arrived.

On May 15th Fan informed us that "Pretty soon now, my believe, ice go away." Jim had gone up a creek to try for fish; when he returned, with a string of suckers he had speared, he agreed with what Fan had said, adding that he believed next day we should "no more ice see."

It was so. When we turned out the following morning, instead of a field of rotting ice, which had all sunk we supposed, there was before our camp a lovely blue lake, sparkling and rippling in a gentle breeze, and Jim gleefully announced, "Now, bossee, you bet we go ahead aller same steamboat."

At once we loaded our raft, and we four drifted on it down the Windy Arm, Tagish Lake. It is but a narrow strip of water, this arm, more like a river. The hills on both sides are steep, the wind from the east rushes through, sometimes dangerously, but we were fortunate to have merely a fresh breeze behind us.

By towing from the shore sometimes, at others by poling, we contrived on the third day to reach the lake, and here we were lucky enough to find not only the men we had heard were cutting lumber there, but that they had just finished a boat which they could sell to us.

These men welcomed us very heartily: they told us we were the first party on the way since the previous autumn. They had run out of tobacco.

The boat they had to sell was not built for either speed or beauty, but we saw it was the very thing for us—it would carry us well with our heavy load to Dawson City. We agreed to their price, which was naturally high, and before we turned in that night we had stowed our goods on board her, and were ready to begin our journey in earnest. We had received a good bit of information about it from these men, who had been often up and down the Yukon. We left them a little happier for our visit, for we had supplied them with a few stores, and notably with tobacco.

We sailed off cheerfully next morning down Lake Tagish. At the mouth of Windy Arm are islands and high mountains,—one superb dome-shaped giant stands alone.

We trolled that day, and caught one large fish like a salmon,—it probably was a land-locked one. Its flesh was white and absolutely tasteless, but Jim and Fan considered it was prime. We made a lovely camp that night on an island near shore.

It took us till the following afternoon to get down this lake. We saw no human beings, but along the sluggish river which joins it to Lake Marsh we passed Tagish House, and there was a group of Indians at which Jim and Fan were terribly alarmed, declaring that if they were seen they would be killed by them, for it appears that war between the Tagishes and the Sticks, which our two were, is perpetual.

Accordingly we gave these Indians a wide berth. Tagish House is but a rough log affair. Yet it is famous, for it is not only the place the tribe meets at annually for its council and festival, but it is the only permanent building in all that country.

Passing down for half-a-dozen miles, we entered Lake Marsh, which occupies a broad valley with high mountains on the east. It is about two miles wide. Traversing it, we got all the wildfowl and the fish we could consume. We lived sumptuously. The journey took us two days.

Fan and Jim were always bright and cheery, and ready to lend a hand; they were good companions, and were uncommonly good specimens of Indians. One particularly good thing about them was that Fan had been taught the use of soap at Metlakahtla, and she had taught her husband; so they were, wonder of wonders, clean Indians!

The foot of Marsh Lake we found to be low and swampy; the sleughs appeared to be full of ducks and musk-rats—also of *mosquitos!*

We certainly expected these last. We had suffered from them in Manitoba and in other parts of Canada; we supposed we knew what we had to contend with, but we did not.

Fortunately we had brought some mosquito netting, which we rigged up in our tent, so that, inside, we had a trifle of peace; but when travelling or moving outside, it was impossible to protect ourselves, and we experienced **untold** misery. Our Indians suffered quite **as much** as we did, and complained as loudly. **They** lit fires inside their tepee, filling it with pungent smoke, through which they slept contented; but we could not stand that.

I may here say that from this time on, with **very** rare exceptions, we were simply tortured by mosquitos. We passed through many hardships, had innumerable physical difficulties to contend with **during that** summer and winter, but they are all forgotten, **or regarded as** mere trifles, and one phase of misery is vividly recorded on my memory: it is the ceaseless torment of those infernal **gnats**. **They are** the cause of the worst suffering that people must submit to in that country: **winter's** cold, summer's heat, even hunger, are **not to be compared** to this awful pest.

For instance, you **are** tramping with a load upon your **back,** your hands are full carrying tools **or** packages, **the sun** is blistering hot, the perspiration is pouring off **you in** streams, yet **all the time the** ubiquitous mosquitos are engaging **your closest** attention; your eyes, your ears, **your** nostrils, all your most sensitive spots, are **their** favourite feeding-grounds. **You** are helpless, **you suffer** agony, and you often feel that life **itself is next** thing to a curse. **We** have seen hardy, rough men shed tears **of** impotent anger at these innumerable, invisible, relentless enemies. Dogs and men, cattle and wild beasts, deer especially, and even bears, are their victims.

Frequently we were so swollen about our necks that we could hardly turn our heads, and our wrists were so enlarged that our wristbands were useless. We tried tobacco juice, turpentine, lamp-oil, but nothing gave us relief. Truly the mosquitos of the Yukon hold the record as tormentors.

Lake Marsh is twenty miles long. It then narrows, and for nearly thirty miles we followed the course of the river, which is the Lewes. The current is about three miles an hour, and we were blessed with a gentle breeze astern, so got on famously. We passed through miles and miles of cut sandbanks, which were completely honeycombed by a species of martin, which were then busy nesting. The air was alive with millions of these little birds, and we gloried in the knowledge that they were feeding exclusively on our deadly foes.

Here we met with a few large salmon. They come all the long way up from Behring Sea to spawn. In August, Jim said, the river is crowded with them, and the bears come down from the hills to feed on them. Dozens, he assured us, might be seen any day along that river. We saw but one; we shot at and missed it.

Up to this time, it will be noticed, we had experienced only fine weather,—indeed, so far, our only real suffering had been from the mosquitos; but one evening, the sun being high, though it was ten P.M., the sky was suddenly enveloped in dense clouds, against which steamlike scud drifted with great rapidity; and by the action of the martins and water-fowl, and by the sudden cessation of the rapacity of the mosquitos, which had been earlier in the day more persistent than usual, we knew that some change was at hand.

Jim said that wind was coming, so we camped, put our tents up with extra care, and drew our boat into what we thought was a safe harbour by the river side.

Not long after—we could see up stream for at least a mile—we perceived that a huge wave was bearing down to us. It was like a bore. We stared aghast!

Our boat and nearly all we had was in imminent danger. I made a rush, intending to leap on board, push it out into the river, then turn its head to the great surge that was rolling down, and so, I hoped, save it from wreck; but Meade held me back, shouting above the dreadful roar of wind and water that I should not go—that the risk was far too great.

As we stood thus, he restraining me, I struggling to go, Jim passed us, stripped: he leapt into the boat, pushed her off, then with one grand sweep of the steering oar he turned her head up stream just as the wave reached her. She lifted with the heave of it, veered this way and that, the heavy water curled up, and we stood there trembling, feeling sure that she would be swamped. But Jim held on manfully, kept her well up, and although she was carried down stream at terrible speed, yet we saw that the brave Indian, standing like a bronze statue at the stern, had conquered.

It was soon lost to sight in the gloom, for the spray which the mighty wind raised was driving down river as if it were drifting snow.

So far, the boat, we trusted, had escaped, but what would ultimately become of her and Jim, we wondered.

We turned to Fan, asking what she thought about it. She was crouched under the lee of a log, smiling peacefully!

"No you bother," she shouted, "Jim all light; outfit all light too. By'me by, pretty soon, no mo' wind, Jim tie up er boat, come back'n we pack all tings down to boat—or, mebbee, Jim bring boat back here. You see me?—well, all light!" and she smiled again quite happily.

How we blessed our stars that we had hired this Indian and his charming klootchman. We thought her a perfect heroine that night, whilst I believe she considered us very childish for being so very much alarmed.

Almost as quickly as this heavy squall had arisen it ceased, the sun streamed out, and the silence was oppressive, yet very welcome. But what should we do about Jim?

We consulted Fan, who calmly replied, "Nosing, nossir, make muck-a-muck, what you call supper, then turn in, my tink Jim come along all lightee by'me by, soon."

At which we made up the fire, and did as she advised.

We were aroused towards morning by Jim calling to his wife from the other side the river. He told us that the boat was safely moored a mile below, that he had tried to bring her to camp but could not, therefore we must pack all to her. He swam across and joined us, after which we had our first real essay at "packing," and we concluded that it was not our forte. We found our boat and her cargo safe and sound below, which was no small blessing. It took two days to pack all down to her. Then on we went again, the stream carrying us along between smooth grassy hills and sandy knolls. Soon the current became stronger, and we heard a distinct roar ahead, and on the bank we saw a board stuck up by some friendly voyageur, on which was scrawled in big letters—"*Danger, Stop,*" which at once we did.

We had arrived at Myles Cañon, the grand cañon of the Lewes—the Miners' Grave.

Eager to examine what we had now to encounter, Meade and I landed and went ahead to prospect. Where we had stopped the river was two hundred yards wide at least: it was roaring ahead in the middle, rushing vehemently on its way.

We mounted the basalt cliff above where we were camped, and came in full view of the cañon. We knew the length of it and the width, we had heard so much about it, and believed we knew just what to expect, yet the reality appalled us. How could we get through? It looked impossible: still, knowing that it had been done, and if we were to reach our destination we must negotiate it, we sat on an outstanding point and wondered.

The walls of the gorge, which averages one hundred feet in width, are about the same height; they are worn into fantastic shapes, very little vegetation clings to them, but along the top there is timber, and one can march through it with ease.

The river, forced through this narrow cañon, is heaped up in the middle much higher than at the sides: it is one mass of foam, and it flashes along at lightning speed, roaring and raging. It is about three-quarters of a mile from fairly smooth water up stream to quietness below.

As we sat on the summit of the cliff, critically examining the scene, we presently perceived two tents at what looked to be the lower end of the gorge, and there was the smoke of a camp-fire.

With Jim and Fan, who had joined us, we consulted; it resulted in Meade and Jim going ahead to visit these campers and obtaining information. From them they learned that they had got through safely. There were half-a-dozen men, old Yukoners, friendly and communicative, who had wintered by Lake Marsh, where they had got a little gold. They offered to help us. Some of them returned and packed each a load over the portage, and then as they saw that neither of us was experienced at shooting rapids, one of them very kindly volunteered to go through with Fan and Jim in our boat.

Everything was carefully planned, the strength of the steering sweep tested; Jim stripped, Fan doffed all she could decently, and our new friend, whom his chums called Samson, did the same,—then the start was made.

Meade stayed to push them off; I went to the cliff-top to watch the proceedings.

Fan and Samson took the oars, Jim was steersman. They pulled far out into the eddy, straining every nerve, even after the current caught them, so as to keep steerage way on the boat. They soon shot into the dark shadows of the walls. Here, they told us, they were nearly stopped by the first huge breaker, but only for a second: the frail boat trembled, seemed to stagger, then surmounting the crest, dashed on.

I, on the top, could mark their progress easily. I saw them flying like a cork through the turmoil; I saw them now whirled one way, now another; at one moment it seemed they were to be hurled against the adamantine walls, where they would be stove to

SHOOTING MYLES CAÑON.

splinters instantly; at the next they miraculously sheered away into the boiling turmoil in the midst. Clouds of spray dashed over them; they were often lost to my sight. Half a minute passed—I saw their speed slacken—was anything wrong? No, I saw they were in the eddy, and were half-way through; next moment they were again in the thick of it, and, so far as I could tell, they were having more terrible experiences still. There were then a few indescribable moments. I held my breath, as I am sure they did theirs, as they vanished from my sight round an intervening point.

Directly after one of our new acquaintances at the camp below fired two shots and waved a red blanket, the signal agreed on that all was well.

From the moment they started until I saw that signal was exactly two and a half minutes by my watch.

With thankful hearts we two shouldered our light packs, crossed the portage, and joined the others. Jim and Fan were perfectly unconcerned,—he was contentedly smoking beside the fire, she was putting our tent up. We thanked Jim, called him a brave good fellow, at which he merely grunted "Ugh"; and Fan said, "Orl right—welly good; guess we make camp here one day—eh?"

We were agreeable to this, especially as the other party was remaining too. They were Canadians, very decent fellows indeed, and on that and for several days we kept company with them with much mutual pleasure.

On the river-side were several mounds, marked with rough stones or wooden crosses. They were the graves of some of the many who had lost their lives there—many more had been drowned whose bodies had never been recovered—and we, I hope, were very grateful that we had got through so safely.

Next day a couple of us went ahead in one of their light canoes to examine the White Horse Rapids—they were two miles on—and to arrange how to attack them. Then we loaded our boats, and, by warping and towing, we, by degrees, hauled them to a place where there is slack water, just above the dangerous place.

Here we camped again, unloaded everything, and hauled boats and canoes on shore. Then we carried our packages on to smooth water below, and lastly dragged the boats there: there were many willing hands to help now, and we did it all quickly.

These rapids are full of sunken rocks, impossible to steer amongst. There is one piece particularly formidable: it is only about one hundred feet, and has been shot, but not intentionally up to that time. With light well-made canoes it would be possible, we thought, though very risky, but with the really unwieldy boat of ours it was impossible.

When we had everything safely over—it took us

best part of a day, and we all worked very hard to do it—we packed up again, and camped for the night. We had a most jovial evening—there was a banjo in the crowd, and one good singer, the weather was grand, the mosquitos were rather less troublesome than usual, and the last great obstacle had been thus safely mastered. Yet there were many graves about us of poor fellows who had failed where we had come through with such success.

Next morning early we were off again.

We had now reached the place to which Jim and Fan had agreed to accompany us. We were loath to part with them, and, so far as we could judge, they were not anxious to leave us. If good food and plenty of tobacco is an Indian's idea of earthly bliss, then I should think these two had all they could desire. I must say they appeared to appreciate it, and when we spoke to them about returning to the coast they were evidently anything but pleased.

Besides, how were they to go back? We had really never thought of that: it was very stupid of us. We had brought their sled, but they could not go home on that.

We should have brought a canoe with us. We proposed to buy one from the Canadians, but they would not part with one.

Jim showed no anxiety at all to solve the problem; as for Fan, she declared her intention was to go on to Dawson City in our company! but this she said merely to tease Jim. The fact is, they were both perfectly satisfied with the life, and indifferent about returning to Skagway, where what they call their home was thought to be. They talked about Lake La Barge, the Five Fingers, and the Rink in such a way that we believed they did really intend to come with us, whether we would or not, if they could.

It ended in our proposing to continue Jim in our employ until we reached our journey's end, offering him the same pay—that is, one dollar a day and food, now, for himself and Fan.

They had been very quiet and melancholy for some hours: when we made this proposal they jumped up, laughed, and shouted with delight. These Indians are very much like children.

We were very glad too, and, as Meade always said when any question about expense arose between us, "Don't bother; when we get to the spot I know about, we can wash out what will cover all these outlays in twenty minutes!"

CHAPTER III.

From the foot of White Horse Rapids to the head of Lake La Barge the Lewes river is said to be thirty miles. Midway it is joined by the Tahkeena, and runs then through a wide valley, having cut many channels, so that we found difficulty in keeping the right one. The current and the wind were still with us.

We camped together with the Canadians: they had two good boats and two canoes. We should have been a merry party, but for the mosquitos. We caught plenty of fish; in every creek were trout and grayling; they rose to a fly, to a black feather, or even to a scrap of cloth. We trolled when moving, catching white fish and some salmon, proving that no one need starve there at that time of the year.

We were fortunate with our guns, shooting many ducks and geese, several swans, and a few grouse— probably ptarmigan. It was the breeding season, yet we considered we were justified in killing what we needed for our larder. Humming-birds were quite numerous, flitting about the brilliant flowers which were everywhere. We saw ravens, some magpies exactly like English ones, and several bald eagles.

We only shot one deer. At one of our camps a herd of some dozens trotted past. All guns were instantly brought to bear, but as only one contained a ball, but one animal fell. It was a caribou, very much like a reindeer.

We saw a few bears, black and brown, and there were small ones called silver-tips, as they have white throats and chins. Our friends assured us they were fierce, and attack a man " on sight "; but we fancied this was only a hunter's yarn, until we had proof that it is true. This was what occurred :—

We were settled for the night in an exposed position, away from stagnant water and bushes, as we found such spots a trifle freer than others from mosquitos. All of us but Fan were scattered, fishing or trying in the woods for birds, quite free from apprehension of anything untoward happening. It was a beautiful night; the sun had set—that is, it had just dipped behind some mountains to the north; the sky was brilliant in purple, gold, and crimson fire, as it would remain till three or four next morning, when we were to move on again. It was late, eleven, I suppose, and we were all out of sight of camp, when Jim and I—we were after ptarmigan—heard the crack of a rifle there.

"M'm," says Jim, "guess dat Fan ketch'm deer mebbe—welly good shot dat klootchman."

I merely said that I hoped it was so, for he and I were having bad luck, and were longing for meat; fish was palling on us. A few seconds after we heard another shot.

"M'm," says Jim again, "my tink Fan got two deer; zat is welly good."

He had hardly ceased speaking when we heard a third report, and several at quick intervals, at which I said, "Come, we'd better return and help her," and we hastened back to camp.

When we came in sight of the river and our boats, we heard Fan calling. It did not sound as if she were afraid, and yet we realised that she was in earnest; so we hurried, and perceived her on a great log that lay stretched across a narrow chasm in the cliff behind the tents, some distance from the ground. There she stood, firmly planted, with a rifle, looking intently at one spot below her. We called; she looked at us delighted.

"Come on! quick, quick!" she cried. "My have got one silver-tip thar; it is no dead, look out; but my tink he no can move! My cannot see him no more, frow rocks in dere," and she pointed. "My have nosing hyar to frow!"

At which, of course, we began to bombard the spot, and as nothing stirred, we stepped forward slowly, cautiously, till amongst some tangle we found the beast lying dead. Telling Fan this, we called to her to come down.

She walked to the butt end of the log and looked up, then to the other. "My can't!" she cried, half laughing.

"Well, but how did you get there?" I asked.

"My jumped down. My no can get up no more, and my no can come down!"

Jim began haranguing her in Indian, then said that we must cut a pole to reach to the log, which we did, and the girl climbed down and joined us.

Meade and the others had returned during this operation, which we carried out amidst much laughter. The bear was hauled out, dragged to camp, Jim set to work, and we soon had steaks frying for supper—or breakfast was it? We praised Fan for what she had done; she said it was "Oh, nosing—nosing at all, at all!" that the bear was trying to get a salmon we had hung in a bush, and she went for it.

"But how did you get up where you were?" we asked.

She said that the bear drove her there, at which we made her tell exactly what had happened, which she did, with many laughs, much as follows:—

"My was making slapjacks for de supper; my was at de fire. My see de bar a-grabbin' for de fish, and my go for him. My got no gun, no nosing but de fry-pan. You bet my go for him wis zat. Oh, yes! but de bar he no scart; nossir, he come for me; yessir, 'n I go for de tepee, 'n zare I ketch Jim's lifle and katlidges. Well, de bar he come zare too, 'n he went for de tepee—see," and she pointed to where it had been torn. " He make to drag down de tepee 'n ketch dis Injun gal; yessir, 'n so my shoot at him 'n hit him, 'n den my run avay! Oh yes, my run up dat rock dare, 'n de bar kum arter me, 'n he druv me to de aige of de bank dere. 'N he druv, 'n druv, 'n my shot two times— tree times, 'n my guess my didn't hit him bad; 'n he comed up so clost my tink he'd have me. So zen my look down onct; my see de log, my jump for it, 'n when my get dere zat bar he make to come to me too! Yessir, but zat time my get steady shot, my give it him in de tum-tum 'n he go tumblin' down—way down dere where you find him. Oh, you bet, dat last time my shot it hurt him—eh?" Then she turned to her cookery as calmly as if it had been the neck of a pigeon she had wrung, and nothing more.

After this we took care that no one was left alone at camp again, and if by any chance we came across a silver-tip we steered clear of him.

Barring mosquitos—and they were a bar and no mistake—it was a glorious trip down Lewes river: we did it in two days to Lake La Barge.

This lovely sheet of water is five, and in some places ten, miles broad, and about thirty-five long. Our friends parted from us here, and we were left to pursue our travels alone. They could sail straight down the lake, their boats being good and not laden like ours. We dared not venture, as it was blowing stiffly, and there was some sea on.

We followed the coast closely, and were three days doing the journey.

When we left this—the last of the lakes—we found the Lewes had quickened its current to six miles an hour. It was extremely crooked, too, and filled with boulders, causing us much difficult and anxious work; but by means of ropes from shore, and careful poling, we made a safe and fairly rapid progress.

The hills came down, often, sheer to the water's edge, and were generally well timbered. We moved on, mostly at night—that is, when the sun was low: at other times it was too terribly hot, and we found it better to turn night into day.

About twenty-eight miles from Lake La Barge the Hootalinqua river enters from the east: it is as wide as the Lewes at the junction. Here we came in sight of several tents, with people about them. We were for passing unnoticed, for Jim and his wife were terribly afraid of Indians. However, we were hailed from the shore, and begged to land. They were miners, rough customers; but they treated us well, and were glad of the latest news from the outer world. They were Americans. They said they were finding " flour" gold on all the bars, and advised us to stay and prospect; but we made

LAKE LA BARGE.

excuses and hurried on, giving our destination as Fort Cudahy. I believe these men thought we were Government officials, and not gold-seekers, for our equipment was so perfect, and the careless way in which we spoke of gold deceived them.

Cut clay banks, full of martins, were common along this river. We found first-rate camping places, and were never without fish and game, but rarely missed mosquitos for more than an hour or two in the early morning.

Thirty miles below the Hootalinqua the Big Salmon joins. We saw no one about here, though we had heard that its bars carry much gold. Salmon were crowding up its rather shallow mouth when we passed; we could have secured a boatful in an hour with a net.

Below the Big Salmon the hills are high and round, mostly wooded to their summits. Thirty-five miles below, the Little Salmon river enters also from the east. There was a band of veritable Indians fishing. We had much ado to pacify our two—they wished us to keep close to the opposite shore, and generally to act as if we had something to conceal; but we made them sit out of sight, and sailed merrily by, with only the cheery response to our cry, "Klahowya!"[1] from them.

[1] "Clark, how are you?" is the greeting Sir James (then Mr) Douglas used to his second-in-command many years ago, which the Indians caught up, and it is to this day the form of greeting between whites and reds on the Pacific coast.

Still a little farther we passed a camp. A boat was hauled up, the tents were closed; we concluded they were all asleep—it was bed-time anyway.

Twenty miles below this we came to a trading-post kept by one George M'Connel. There was a log-house and store, two or three rough shanties, and a boat or two. We hailed some men, "asking if there were any Indians around?" As they said "No," we landed, and spent an hour with them. M'Connel was impressed with our outfit, and the fact that we had two Indians as helpers struck him as very stylish. He, too, evidently supposed we were on some Government business. We got from these people information about the Five Fingers Rapids, which we had now to tackle.

A short distance below the Little Salmon we passed the Eagle's Nest, which is the most conspicuous landmark along the Lewes. It is about five hundred feet high, rising abruptly from a gravel flat. The river is here three hundred yards wide, and we had come three hundred miles from tide-water at Skagway.

We camped here and tried some of the soil for gold, as we had done at many of our stopping-places. More often than not we got the colour—that is, a few fine specks. In several spots we got so many that we felt sure it would some day pay to work, but Meade always smiled and said, "Don't bother; we'll get all we want directly."

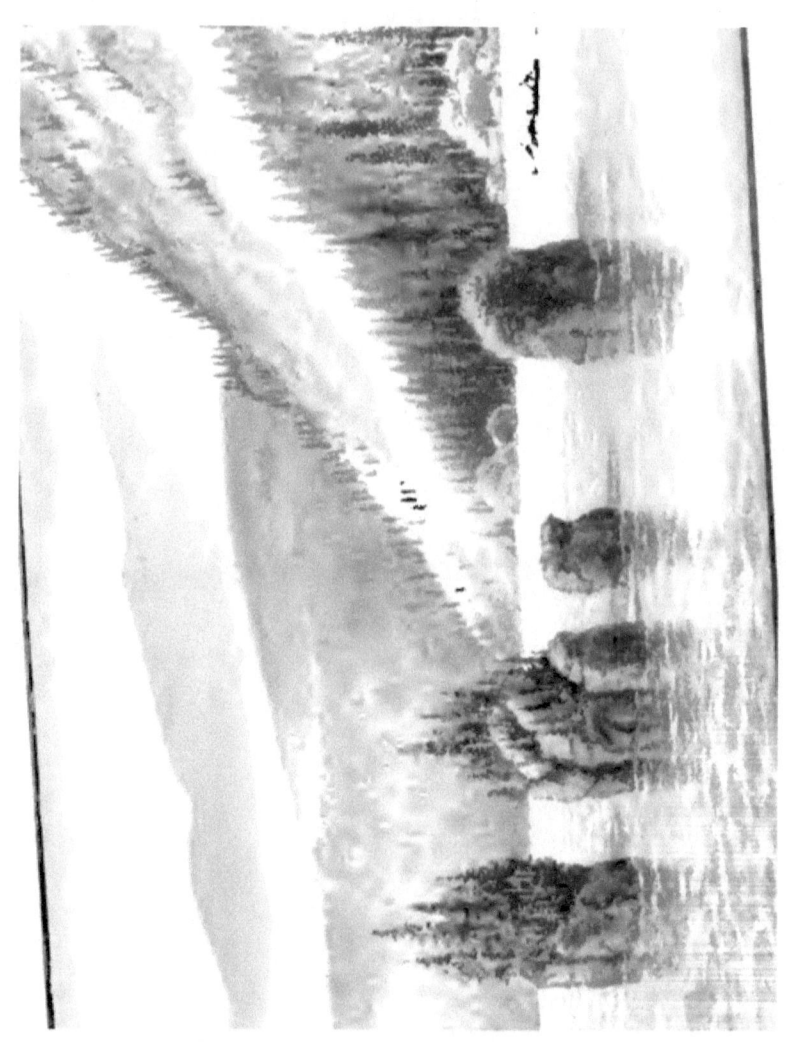

From here the banks are high, of clay and gravel; the current is about five miles an hour. The country was well wooded; there were many birch trees. We had fifty-three miles to go from Little Salmon river, which took us two days only; then Five Fingers came in sight. We had little difficulty in running these rapids—Meade and I had become expert with oars and paddles. We rested for a few hours above them, on the western bank of the river, where he made a sketch, as he had done when any particularly interesting bit was noted and the mosquitos would give him a chance. Then, without discharging any cargo, with Jim at the steering sweep, we ventured forth, crossed to the right-hand shore, into the white water, and in a very few minutes had rushed through the passage, and were in quiet beyond, and the last serious obstruction had been overcome.

We ran on cheerily after this, and came to a bar of rocks they call Rink Rapids, which we passed without mishap. Below this the river widens considerably, and there are many islands, which became more numerous as we advanced: it was often difficult to tell which were the real shores. Past there the high hills came down abruptly to the water, the current was accelerated, and navigation, though not dangerous, needed constant care.

Fifty-five miles from Five Fingers the great Pelly river joins the Lewes, and the two become the Yukon.

Here is old Fort Selkirk, a trading-post of some importance, and there they winter the steamer P. B. Weare, which navigates the Yukon between there and Fort St Michael. Several dwellings and a store were on the bank; half-a-dozen men were about and some women. We supposed they were prospectors, for they spoke of nothing but gold, which indeed was the one topic with every one. Indeed, Gold! Gold! Gold! was in everybody's mouth we met, though certainly they were not numerous.

One man here was very friendly, lavish with advice, telling us again and again about the good places he knew, and saying he only wished he was free to go — he would quickly make his pile and quit the country; at which the bystanders smiled, and winked at one another. One of them told us aside that it was well known that this man had already got better than a gold mine, and was making his fortune rapidly. All the goods he sold were exorbitant in price—which was, as they admitted, fair enough—and everything was paid for in gold dust, which he had to weigh himself. "'N you bet," as an old Yankee miner said with a grin,—" you bet he don't lose much every time he uses them scales o' his'n."

The furs he bought from the trappers and Indians at a very low price, which he paid in goods. Oh, yes; we readily understood he did not need, or really wish, to go gold-mining.

There was a large number of dogs about this place, principally mongrels, yet there were some pure Huskies—that is, Esquimaux dogs. One fine young one had been petted, which made the others jealous: they set upon him whenever they caught him outside alone, which made his owner believe they were bound to kill him, so he offered him to us and we accepted him. We named him Patch, after an old dog I knew in England: we fed him well, and he quickly became a most beautiful and faithful creature—one of the most intelligent dogs I ever knew.

Very little remains of Fort Selkirk now beyond the ruins of the chimneys. It was raided and burned by coast Indians in 1852.

Ninety-six miles on we passed the mouth of the White river, which is of great volume, coming into the Yukon with a roar. It is so called from a white substance it holds in solution, probably volcanic ash. Ten miles below this is the Stewart river, helping to swell the already mighty Yukon. It is deep and dark.

There were a few miners hereabouts. We did not land. They hailed us as we passed, calling out that there was plenty of gold if we would stay and tackle it. We replied that we were bound down river some distance, and one fellow shouted, " Bloomin' Yanks, no doubt!"

Seventy miles below Stewart river we came to another trading-post, and a sawmill actually—this was at Sixty-Mile Creek. We camped below it, as there were some Indians working at the mill, much to Jim's and Fan's horror. Meade and I walked back and purchased some boards to make sluice-boxes, and floated them down to our boat. There were a number of miners about: some spoke favourably of their doings, but most were downhearted, and all looked unhappy. We thought then, and believe it fully now, that mosquitos were the cause of most of it. Here we found to our great content that we had but fifty more miles to run down to the Klondyke. They called it the Thronduk though.

Asking if there was any gold there, we were told not any—that it had been examined well, and there was nothing there to pay. It was just a salmon river and nothing more, at which information Meade looked at me with eyebrows raised and a smile hovering about his mouth.

We heard, however, that twenty miles before reaching that river we should come to Indian Creek, which the year before had proved to be quite rich, though already "played out." But as we heard people were still at work on it, we had doubts about the truth of this. The fact is, gold-hunters are amongst the most easily excited and depressed of beings, and one can rarely depend on individual opinions.

We made the run to the mouth of the Klondyke in two days. Here and there were heaps of ice

ON THE YUKON AT THE MOUTH OF THE KLONDYKE RIVER.

still on the shore and shallows, for it does not entirely disappear from the Yukon till well on in June.

Usually an Indian camp was there, as it is really famous for salmon. They come annually to fish it. Here, too, is Dawson City—described by Meade as a rough miners' camp of shacks and shanties only—chiefly saloons, drinking-bars, dance-houses, and gambling dens. There were only a few hundred people in it, storekeeping and trading with the miners, of whom there were always a number hanging about, spending their hard-earned gold. Our aim being to avoid all communication with the shore, we held back till midnight, when there was a certain gloom spread over the scene, and when most people would be asleep. We were fortunate enough to slip into the river without any notice being taken. There was no very strong current down the Klondyke, yet as we had to pull against it we moved slower: however, finding a sequestered nook a few miles up, we camped before it was what we called day. This stream is not wide. The water is very clear. It was a very beautiful scene, but truly we took no time to criticise our surroundings. We had all we could do to attend to our business, and fight mosquitos!

Naturally we were impatient to reach Meade's last year's camp unobserved, and to discover if his find had been unmolested by wandering prospectors.

We had seen so few human beings about that we hoped for the best; yet, now that we were so near the end of our long journey, we were in a fever of excitement.

Meade and I realised what a mistake we had made in not bringing a light canoe with us, for he knew it would be impossible to get our heavy boat past the rough water at the mouth of the creek where he had found the gold. We could manage our packs, but we four could not convey that boat over the portage.

Besides, how were Jim and his wife to get home? We did not intend to keep them with us whilst we were mining. We firmly believed that they were both true and trustworthy, but they were simple, and it would be easy for them to be led to disclose where we were and what we were doing, so we had determined that they should go back as soon as they had helped us with our stuff on to the still water of Meade's creek.

To carry out our plans, then, we must have a canoe, so it was in the end arranged that I should march into Dawson and, if possible, buy one. It was a difficult tramp, but I managed it.

My arrival at the "City" attracted little notice: a number of men had lately come up by the boat from Fort-St Michael—they supposed I was one of them. I announced that I was one of a party camped up stream, and wanted a canoe.

There was a variety on sale. I don't suppose those who said they owned them did so really—they had been brought there by people who had gone back and abandoned them; but anyway one was offered with a pair of paddles for one hundred dollars—a Peterborough canoe, therefore a good one. I purchased it, got a square meal, and then towards evening I paddled off, not heading up the Klondyke but across it, as if I were going to ascend the Yukon. I wished to put the people off my scent.

I need not attempt to describe what I saw at Dawson. It was rough, and the goings on were rougher. I was assured that there was very little actual crime—only gambling, drinking, and every description of dissipation. There were some women, strange specimens. I came across the wife of a store-keeper, however, who was very pleasant. She was an Englishwoman from Eastbourne. She spoke bitterly of everything there — climate, people, and mosquitos. She admitted that she and her husband were making money, and hoped that a year or two only of the awful life would have to be endured ere they could return to England.

Not having seen or spoken to a decent white woman since I left the steamship at Juneau, I confess it was pleasant to have a talk with this nice Englishwoman, and I am thankful that I made her acquaintance then, as subsequent events will demonstrate.

I did not get back to our camp till the following day, when we started again. We made no rapid progress—there were many shallow bars or ledges to cross; we got stuck more than once, until we put some of our cargo into the canoe and towed her. It took us four days, hard work too, to get up to the rapids at the mouth of what we called "The Creek."

On the way we passed the mouths of several creeks where a few miners were camped. They hailed us, but were so intent upon making use of every moment of the short summer that they really took small heed of us. However, for the last two days we had not seen a soul.

Meade knew the way perfectly. When we reached the rapids we unloaded everything, and carried all with the canoe up to calm water above. The boat we câched in a convenient crevice we found in a rocky bluff near at hand. Then loading all we possibly could into the canoe, my friend and I pushed up stream, paddling, as you may be sure, our very hardest, scarcely taking time to eat or sleep.

We left Jim and his wife in charge of the rest of the stores. We would not allow them to erect tent or tepee. They were to make themselves a wigwam of brush, and to cover all our stuff with bushes, for we did not wish to attract attention, you understand.

I told Jim he might try for gold whilst they

were waiting for our return—that it would be good if he could take some back to the coast; and Fan, laughing merrily, said, "Plenty chickamin (gold) hyar, my will make pile hyar, my feel it in my tum-tum."

These Indians well understood what a pile meant, but their notion of its amount, and what to do with one when they had secured it, were very funny.

On the second night, after having come, as we thought, about forty miles, behold Meade and I hauling our canoe to shore and arrived at our journey's end. For some hours before my companion had been greatly excited. "See that stump?" he would cry. "Yes." "Well, I did that. I camped in there one day."

A little farther on he pointed to a bank covered with brush. "See that bare place there?" "Yes." "Well, I tried a pan of stuff there, and got a good show. I was half a mind to stay on and give it a good examination. I'm glad enough I did not."

From a considerable distance he declared he could see the dug-out which he had made, and where he had passed some weeks; and as we drew quite near he exclaimed with delight, "All's right. I don't believe a living thing has been here since I left last September. Hurrah!"

We had been forty-five days on the journey in. Considering all things, we had done well. It was now, we believed, the third day of July, but we were

E

not certain. We had endeavoured to keep a log of our voyaging, but from there always being daylight now, and from the irregularity with which we had eaten and slept, we were not very sure even of the day of the week!

CHAPTER IV.

In a bank near the creek, which was about twenty yards wide and had a fairly swift current, there was a rough door, which, being half open, disclosed a dark cave within. One sees similar places in railway cuttings and cliffs in Britain, where workmen keep their tools.

In this "dug-out" Meade had lived.

A few cut stumps, some wood chopped for fuel, and the ground bared around this door, were the only indications of any person having ever been about.

There was a quantity of timber growing around, but no really large trees; all were of the fir tribe. The earth was, as usual, covered with moss some feet in thickness, much of it pink and golden, and very beautiful. From the lower branches of trees hung long streamers of gray lichen; rotting logs, dead branches, and rock were cushioned in brilliant mosses, green and orange, whilst creepers and bushes were thickly matted everywhere. Yet, as we well knew, beneath this and for many feet below it the ground was frozen, in spite of the sun's great heat, which could not penetrate that mass of vegetation.

There we were, then, entirely alone, so far as we could tell, many miles from any one but Jim and his klootchman. Yet we thought it better, in spite of this belief, not to put up our white tent: some wandering prospector might come our way, and it was better not to attract attention, therefore we decided to enlarge this dug-out and dwell in it.

Fancy a hole scooped out of the bank about ten feet square, very little higher than a man, with a hole in one corner of the roof to allow the smoke from the fire to escape: that was all, and that was to be our home—for three months, we said.

How little we knew what was before us!

The front of this luxurious habitation was built up with logs, the chinks between stuffed with moss; the door was of rough split slabs; it had no hinges—to open and close it one had to lift it bodily. There were a few notches in the top which admitted all the light we had when it was shut.

The remains of Meade's last year's bedding (fir twigs), a few old tins, and bits of rubbish, strewed the floor. It was just a den, and a very dismal one at that,—far worse than the meanest hopper's crib in Kent.

First we lit a big fire inside, and when the frost was driven out we set to with pick and shovel and very quickly enlarged it by about five feet, after which we strewed a thick layer of fresh pine brush over the floor, spread our bedding, and were at home!

"It'll do," said Meade; "we can exist here till we've got all the gold we want — that will not take long, you'll see. Then for England, home, and beauty, eh?"

I said, "All right, it's good enough for me."

We made a pot of tea, boiled part of a salmon we had taken just before we landed—the creek appeared to be full of them—then we rolled ourselves in our blankets, tired out, and I soon slept in spite of dirt and heat.

The sun was high when I was awakened by my companion, who called me excitedly. He held a tin pannikin in his hand. "See," he exclaimed; "it was a shame to rouse you, but I could not help it. I went down to the bar and got a pan of dirt, and this is what I have washed out of it!" and he held the tin close to my face, and there was a handful of gold in it, dust and small nuggets—bright, shining, yellow nuggets, looking like pieces of shelled walnuts which had been gilded!

"Now, Bertie, what d'ye say?" he went on, as I stared at the gold, took some up and let it run through my fingers; "are you sorry you have come? Isn't all we have gone through a mere nothing? isn't it all forgotten?—and there's heaps and heaps of it!"

I was on my feet now. I could not say I was amazed, for I had heard so much about it from my friend, and had learned to trust his words so implicitly; but I was pleased, I was delighted, in fact, to find that he had not been mistaken, and that we had not come up to this dismal place and passed through all our hardships in vain. Indeed it was grand, and I said so.

We hardly had patience to wait for the kettle to boil. We swallowed some breakfast in a hurry, then with shovel and tin dish we each went at it, and we worked away till we judged that it was noon, out on a gravelly point that jutted into the stream close to the shanty.

As we moved this gravel we could *see* the gold; no wonder Meade had brought out what he did—it was easy to do it. I picked out several handfuls myself that morning, and so did he, and this, with what we washed out, weighed over fifty ounces!

We had thus proved that all was right. I had myself seen it, handled it, washed it, picked it out. Naturally we were both highly elated.

It was hard to drag myself away from all this, but I had to. I took a blanket and a little grub, got into the canoe, and paddled off down the creek. I was returning to Jim and his wife to bring up the rest of our property. Jim was to return with me; Fan was to remain there until her husband came down with the canoe which we had given them, then they were to get back to the headquarters of their band.

Meade had said farewell to them already, now I had to do so. It was not a pleasant business, for we had both become really attached to these two Indians, and I am sure that the liking was mutual. We had found them perfectly trustworthy and reliable, and very different in their habits and, so far as we could judge, in their ideas, to what we had always supposed were characteristic of their race. We had treated them in terms of equality with ourselves; we had shared alike of late, and had learnt much that was useful and interesting from them, and I believe they had learnt some good from us. At any rate, Fan said to me one day, "S'pose all white folk same as you and Meade, there no be so plenty bad Injun"; which was satisfactory.

Paddling energetically, the current with me, I reached their camp the following evening, so fatigued that I slept nearly twelve hours on end! It was noon next day before Jim and I had the canoe loaded and were able to start up stream again.

My leave-taking with Fan was really quite sad: I must admit that I never supposed I could have felt it so. As for the poor girl, she showed no apathy: she shed many tears, and made me certain that if I should ever go to that country again I would find a welcome from Fan, her husband, and her entire nation. True, they had been well treated, and, I suppose for them, well paid. They had a handsome canoe given to them, and many other little things which they valued; but, for all that, I believe their grief at parting from us was quite genuine.

Fan shouted to me as I paddled up stream with her man, "Plenty come again soon; my will be sick by'me-by, all er time, for love of you!"

I did not take Jim right up to our shanty. About a mile below it, where a small stream trickled down a bank, we landed the cargo. I had to make him suppose that it was up there we intended to remain, as we did not wish him to know exactly where we were, and what we were doing. With many a hearty hand-clasp, with many a good wish on both sides, I parted with that Indian. I have never seen him since, nor have I heard of him or his good wife, but the day may come when I shall do so. I believe their association with us did them good, and I know that always in the future, when men speak evil of Indians, I shall adhere to my opinion that there are *some* good and true ones.

I found that Meade had increased our lot of gold during my absence to over one hundred ounces!

After packing in our stores, amongst which were a few tools and a trifle of ironmongery, with which we did a little to our domicile, and having fed and slept, which we considered all but waste of time, we went at gold getting.

It was most absorbing, and, in a sense, glorious work. For over a week we worked with pans and fingers only. A ridge of rock ran across the creek, against which the gravel had been washed by the stream; this formed a bar, and here we were getting the gold, and down on this rock itself, the bed rock, was where we found it richest. By the week-end we had hidden away what was worth one thousand pounds each—some fifty pounds weight of gold!

At the finish of the next we had more than doubled the quantity, and we were reckoning that if we could keep going like that till the middle of September, we should be able to take out ten thousand pounds apiece—five hundred pounds weight of it! We could think of nothing to prevent it.

We had by working, often to our waists, in ice-cold water, got out all the gravel we could from the river; we then began to trace the run of golden dirt in along the rock, which led into the bank a few yards only from our den. We found that it continued quite rich, and so far as we could tell this vein or lead might continue into the hill to an indefinite distance. We removed the moss and vegetation, then raised a huge fire over the spot where we wished to dig; in a few hours the ground was thawed a foot or two; we dug that out, and lit another fire, and thawed a little more. We kept at it thus almost day and night. We were well paid for it, no doubt, so far as getting gold went.

In three weeks we had excavated into the bank ten feet and more, following the streak on bed rock, and found it always rich. We made a dump, or heap of wash dirt, at the entrance. Our piles were in it, we had good reason to feel sure; besides, we had, as we considered, equally rich ground ahead of us.

One thing we knew, that if we should be discovered we could each claim five hundred feet along the creek; indeed, we thought twice that, as discoverers, so that our claim on the Klondyke might be two thousand feet in length. Therefore we need not have been so much afraid of being found. I used to say so to Meade, who invariably replied that we were better as we were, and were bound to keep our secret as long as possible.

It was now the middle of August—we had attempted to continue a sort of diary, but we had quite lost count by this time of dates and days. For weeks there had been no darkness, there was only what the Shetlanders call "the dim," and which we could then perceive was becoming more pronounced. We ate and slept when we felt we must; the rest of the time we worked without ceasing—we took no relaxation whatever.

Our creek was now alive with salmon; we could, with a long-handled shovel, scoop one out whenever we liked. They were so closely packed that they crowded each other out. In places many had been forced on to the land, where they lay rotting by the hundred: crows and ravens, jays, magpies, and hawks were numerous, feeding on dead fish, and several times we noticed bears dragging the salmon out and gorging themselves with them—not one bear only, often we saw several at once catching and eating them, or lying, surfeited with food, on sunny banks asleep.

We could easily have killed all we wished of them, but we did not dream of doing so; we had stores in plenty, as much salmon as we chose— why should we bother about bear meat?

About this time Meade first complained of being out of sorts. He was a powerful man, and had, till lately, looked the picture of health, but now clearly a change had come over him. He was pale, always tired, and did not eat properly. Was it to be wondered at? Such work, such living, such worry with mosquitos would tell on any one.

I, too, felt that I was not the man I should be. Yet in spite of all, we told each other we must stick to it for another six weeks, then we could rest, which was foolishness. One night we both felt so bad that we could neither work nor eat; it had become serious. Then we settled to devote the next few days to making a sluice with the boards we had brought, hoping that change of work, which, it is said, is as good as play, would prove so in our case: it did.

We constructed three-sided boxes, the depth and width of our boards, and about six feet long, an inch or two wider at one end than the other; across the inside, along the bottom, we put bars or riffles a foot apart. We made six of these boxes, then went up stream, where a little obstruction, a sort of dam, raised the water; there we cut a groove, or ditch, and led a powerful stream into the boxes, which we had set up by our dump, one behind the other on a slant, the narrow ends fitting into the wider, so as to form a trough some thirty feet long. This was our sluice.

Into the upper boxes we threw the wash dirt, allowing the water to rush over it. One of us was continually throwing in the dirt, the other stirred it about and flung out the large stones and coarse gravel with a long-handled shovel.

Thus, by degrees, against the riffles was collected fine sand and gold, which once a day we cleared away thoroughly, turning the run of water on one side whilst we did it. This washed stuff we then panned off in the usual way, and a very delightful operation this was, for the amount of gold we got and stored away daily was immense.

By this process we were able to wash a very much larger amount of stuff than before, and we soon had our dump cleared away, and found we had, in old meat tins and bags, not less than three hundred pounds weight of gold!

OUR DUG-OUT, OUR TUNNEL, AND OUR SLUICE.

Feeling much better after this, we stupidly went on working as hard as ever, and in a few days were queer again. Then we realised that this would not do at all, and we determined to take things much easier. We had done splendidly; we could go home with a large sum each, and we believed that we could at Dawson City register, or in some way secure, our claim, and could return to it next season. Or, as we said, we could surely find capitalists in Canada or England to pay us well for such a splendid property. At any rate, we knew we should do well to cease this extraordinary labour, yet every day add something to our pile.

Having by this time driven in a tunnel quite twenty feet, and being at least forty from the surface, we were not troubled with frozen ground, and could work more easily, anyway. It was quite dark in there: we burnt candles, of which we had brought with us a quantity.

We left off work in reasonable time now, we smoked and read and talked and sketched of an evening, and planned what we should do about getting home, and what big things we would do when we had arrived there.

During all this time we had experienced wonderfully good weather. I have no recollection of any rain; we had strong winds and squalls often,—we rather liked them, for they lessened the insect pests, but by the end of August mosquitos had much diminished in numbers. Although we had nightly frosts, some pretty severe, when the sun was high they came in clouds, and sometimes we thought they were more bloodthirsty than ever. And thus, as the time went by, we began to realise that the day was drawing near when we must depart.

We spent a little time now with our guns, killing several deer close to our den. We often saw bears; we left them alone, having plenty of venison.

We had not seen a human being, or the sign of one, since we had been up there. But one morning early, for there was real day and night now—the sun rose about four—I was awakened by low growls from Patch, who happened to be in with us that night. I motioned the dog to be silent, and, listening, I heard footsteps outside. Pit-a-pat they went; then I heard a bucket being moved.

I reached over and shook my companion gently; when he awoke I whispered, "There's some one about at last."

Meade roused up, listened, and, jumping from his blankets, stepped to our spy-hole. Then, turning to me, he held his finger up for silence, and with a smile motioned me to come and look. I did so; it was a huge bear, the largest I had ever seen, snuffing about, examining things, and it was not ten yards away!

I asked by signs if I should shoot it—for answer Meade handed me my rifle, and I let fly at the beast.

I was altogether too careless, too sure that I should put the ball just where I wanted to. At any rate, I only grazed its skull, and did not even stun it—only aroused its fury, for it turned with a roar of anger, and came at our frail door with a bound.

I jumped back as the door fell inwards, and the huge creature stood for a moment glaring at us. Patch flew at him, barking vociferously.

My other barrel was a smooth-bore, and only held shot; but Meade was ready with his rifle. He fired, hit the bear square between the eyes, and the beast fell prone upon the door. He lifted up his head a time or two, opened his savage mouth, and growled; but he was practically dead and harmless, whilst our good dog mounted on his carcase, howled with excitement, waved his grand tail, proud of victory, probably thinking that he himself had done it.

"By George!" exclaimed Meade, "a splendid fellow, eh? It must be a St Elias grizzly!"

Its fur was brown, long and thick. We took the skin off and stretched it around the butt of a tree, fastening Patch near to keep strange beasts away. As for the meat, we found it excellent for a change. We hoisted a lot of it up into adjoining trees. It was very fat.

The scent of it attracted many animals about us, wolves and wolverines, foxes and lynxes. Patch kept them from doing harm.

The woods were seldom altogether silent at night;

one often heard the howls and barks of many creatures. Foxes were very numerous. There were many silver grey and black ones. We shot them whenever we had the chance: we skinned and stretched them properly, as we had learnt to do in Ontario.

I don't believe that two fellows were ever better fitted to be companions, under such circumstances, than Meade and I were. He was a very cheerful man, always looking at the bright side of things, full of resources, an excellent bushman.

He told me much about his English home, spoke often of his mother, for whom he had the greatest love and veneration. His father had been dead for years. Money was not too abundant with his mother and his two sisters; he was often saying what a blessing the gold that he had got would be to them.

I could tell, too, that there was one person in England around whom all his warmest feelings were centred. He did not say very much to me about her, for, as he knew from me that I was perfectly heart-whole, I believe he thought that I could not sympathise with him, nor understand his feelings. Meade was very well read, and his conversation was always very pleasant. As for me, he was kind enough to say that he could not have had a better "mate."

It was in the beginning of September, our health

was not good, and the season was hurrying towards winter, when we deemed it wise to begin to carry out some plan for getting away. We had not acted wisely, I must admit; that is, we should have arranged as well for getting out as for getting in. How were we to take our camping gear, our grub, and our gold down to our boat?

We should have brought up two canoes with us —one for Fan and Jim to get away in, another for ourselves.

Meade saw this now, and was always blaming himself for the error, saying that as he knew the lie of the land he should have known better.

These points he and I had discussed again and again, and had not really settled what to do, when this time arrived.

Certainly we could not "pack" our stuff. There was no decent trail, and even if there had been, we knew we were not robust enough to take a dozen journeys to our boat and back, heavily laden, as we should have to be. No! By some means we must *float* down to the Klondyke, to the main stream, where our boat was câched.

And about the boat, too, we had some anxiety. Supposing it had been found and carried off, where should we be?

Certainly we had acted most unwisely.

There was a bear track along the creek which it was possible to traverse, and as the existence of our boat was of first importance, we arranged to take a small pack each and go down to ascertain if all were well.

I shall not easily forget that tramp. We were three days reaching the mouth of our creek, but we found our boat safe. We rested there a day, and then marched home again; and such a march that was too! The path was quite narrow, and seldom along level ground—indeed it appeared that the bears preferred to climb boulders, creep along logs, or tramp through the softest sleughs. Bad as the trail was, however, it would have been impossible to get through those woods at all if we had left it.

We saw at least twenty bears on this journey, besides hearing many scooting through the bush. They did not approve of other travellers along their road. They showed no disposition to dispute with us though. They blew and snorted, but fled.

We thus realised how utterly impossible it would be to even carry what gold we had that way, to say nothing of other things we must have with us. Hours were spent discussing these important questions.

When we reached our place we searched the adjacent forest for a cedar or a pine tree big enough to make a dug-out canoe. We felt certain we were axemen enough for that; but, alas! there were no large trees there.

So then, at last, we had to come down to the plan I had favoured from the first. It was that we should build a raft. I knew that we could construct one which we could navigate. **The** stream was not **too rapid,** although crooked, much encumbered with **boulders,** logs, and snags. I had traversed it in the canoe three times; with good luck I believed I could take a raft down too.

We did not intend to take many of the stores **we** still had with us, for it was our determination to return in the spring of '98. All tinned things and many others would keep good in that climate if we protected them from bears **and** other beasts.

The first idea was to stow them **in** our den, making all secure with rocks and timber, but we found this would be too difficult and risky. So we made a câche, as the Indians do to preserve their salmon—that is, high up between two suitable trees near. We built a huge box or safe of logs, large enough to hold **all** we proposed **to** leave behind. The trees **we chose** were not large. Bears **cannot** climb small ones, unless there are plenty of branches to hold by. **We took care** to remove all such helps as **we** came **down from** our task, and **so** felt secure.

Next we turned seriously to building the raft.

Selecting trees for the purpose, we felled and rolled them to the water, notched and pinned them together, fitted others across and across again, carefully lashing all in such **a way** that we felt would be safe. To do this we were working up to our waists in water often, and it was **icy cold.**

I think it was on the third day we had been at this job when Meade took really ill. I know we reckoned that we only had two or three hours more work to complete it when he gave in.

There was only one heavy log to get into position. I said to him that if he could give me a hand with that, I could do the rest alone. Then we would pack up and be off, for I hoped and believed that the change of scene and work, and the actually having started on the long journey out and home, would soon set him to rights.

We were talking thus, and the poor fellow was doing all he could to aid me. He was lifting one end of the log which was to complete the structure; then, whilst I was finishing, he was to go inside, turn in, and try if sleep would help him—when, putting out all his strength to lift, his foot slipped upon a barked stick under water, and he came down heavily, the log he had been lifting falling sharply across his legs!

I shall never forget the look on his face as he sank back slowly in the water, which rippled over him to his waist.

He turned deathly pale, then red; his eyes were dilated, his expression was terrible. "Bertie, Bertie," he groaned, "it is all up with me, my leg is broken!"

As for me, I was appalled; for a few moments I was dumb with fear. I thought my friend would drown!

I suppose I simply stared at him with open mouth; I don't really know what I did, or thought. There was my poor friend pinned to the bottom of the creek by a heavy piece of timber, his head and shoulders only out of water, his hands pressing against that awful log to keep it from rolling farther on to him.

Thank God, though dazed, I was not idle long. I leapt ashore, seized a handspike, got it under the end of the stick, and prised it up quite clear of him. Then I called to him that he was free, and begged him to move away.

But he could not. He repeated that his leg was broken, and that he was jammed there; that if I could not help him he must there lie—there die! He spoke in such a despondent manner, he looked so dreadful; his teeth were chattering with the cold. It was awful.

I was all this time exerting my power to keep the log up, and off him. I realised that I could not do that for long, and if I let go it would go down on him and hurt him worse perhaps. It was a horrible fix to be in. I suppose it lasted hardly twenty seconds, but it seemed to me an hour.

What could I do? How could I, in the first place, get that log entirely clear of him? That was the question. I looked round in despair; would no clever thought come to me? I think in those few seconds I lifted up my heart to God Almighty very earnestly.

Thanks be to Him, He did show me a way. The handspike, or lever, I had was a pole of considerable length. I found that by moving to the end farthest from the log I could with very little pressure keep it up. There were branches and sticks about; with one hand I put enough of them upon the end of the lever to keep it down, when I let go entirely, and wading into the creek beside my friend, who had fainted—he was insensible at any rate—I put out all my strength and pushed the log clear.

As it fell it splashed the water over Meade and brought him to. He looked at me despairing. "Come, come, dear friend!" I cried, "the log is off you; make an effort, let us get you out of this!"

He tried hard, groaning with pain; he really swooned more than once as he endeavoured to drag himself out, and somehow, I cannot remember how, he did get out, and I got him clear and on to a level place on the bank, and then I let him rest whilst I got him some whisky—for we had brought a little with us, "in case of accident," we said, and here was an accident indeed.

After a little while my chum revived. He said the agony in one leg was intense. He was quite unable to help himself or to discuss the situation.

First thing, I was sure, was to get him inside; then we must discover what was really wrong. He declared he knew that his thigh was fractured. The slightest movement made him scream with anguish. Yet moved he must be—but how was I alone to do it? I am a big fellow. I endeavoured to lift him bodily. I could not. His constant cry was, "Let me lie—and die!"

Suddenly an idea occurred to me. We had just been reading about Swiss mountaineering, and that to get wounded people or ladies unable to walk over the ice and snow they use hides, or, failing them, sacking—anything really which is strong enough.

Well, I remembered the bearskin we had—would that do?

I tore it from the tree, spread it out by Meade, the fur side up, then with all the tenderness I could exert I contrived to get it under him: he could help himself but little, and half the time he appeared to be unconscious.

As for my thoughts, I cannot recall them really. If, as he said, his thigh was broken, what could *I* do for him? I had no knowledge at all of surgery. I was almost despairing, and began to fear it would indeed be that he would die!

Good old Patch seemed to realise that some great disaster had occurred. The expression on his face was almost human. He sat perfectly still, intently watching us.

To get Meade in, and lying on his far from comfortable bed, was the first thing to do—of that I was quite sure. It was no easy task. I did, however, manage by attaching a rope to the bearskin to haul him along by degrees, and at last got him near the fire. Still on the bearskin, I arranged him with rugs and blankets, as we had plenty.

Next thing was to examine his hurts. I cut off his boots and clothing. I found one leg was much cut and bruised, but he could move it—it was the other that was seriously damaged. I found that it was broken just above the knee!

Naturally my first thought was that we must have a doctor. But how could it be managed? Could I leave him for a forty-mile tramp to the boat? Could I launch it alone? Could I navigate it alone to Dawson? When I did get there, could I get a doctor to come out with me?

It would take at the very least ten days to go and come, and where would my poor friend be then? He would die indeed without me. He would freeze to death, even if I left food and water handy, for it froze every night, and the earth itself was frozen always, summer and winter, you must remember, and if the fire died out he could not rekindle it.

No—it was impossible. I could not leave him.

We talked this over, at least I talked, and he agreed with me — that we must sink or swim together, that we could not be parted. He was awfully depressed.

I plied him with hot tea and whisky—that is all

I could think of then, and he became calmer after a little. But soon he became uneasy again. "Bertie, dear friend," said he, with a mournful sigh, "I see clearly nothing can be done. I must die here—that is plain."

"Not if I can help it," I declared, and I begged him to tell me what he thought I could do for him; that as it was evident I could not leave him, I must do something—if only to alleviate his pain.

He asked what I knew of surgery, if I had ever seen a leg set, if I thought that I could do it. I was grieved at heart to have to tell him that I was absolutely ignorant about all such matters.

He lay silently for a long time—I thought he slept. I made up the fire, closed the door, lit the lamp, for it was evening, then I sat on the ground beside him, very sorrowful — ay, far more than sorrowful—I was despairing.

A broken leg—no surgeon—no appliances—a fearful journey before us through an Arctic winter, for I knew that at the best many weeks, perhaps months, must elapse before my friend could possibly start homewards, and what could I do alone? I was utterly ignorant about sickness and sick-nursing, and I knew nothing about cooking food suitable for a sick man, even if we had the materials to cook.

There was a long, long silence, only the crackling of the fire in the corner, the sough of the wind amongst the pines outside, or the weird howl of a wolf prowling around our miserable home.

Patch sat upright by the fire, almost motionless. He scarcely shut an eye; he appeared to be full of sad thoughts. Occasionally he turned his head slowly and gazed first at Meade a while, and then at me, and then, as if he too was quite despairing, he gazed long and sorrowfully at the burning wood. Certainly that good dog knew that something terrible had happened to his friends.

CHAPTER V.

It was about midnight before Meade spoke again. He had been lying motionless, though occasionally a low groan escaped him. I thought he had been sleeping, from the effect of the whisky I had given him; however it was not so.

Suddenly, with a cry of anguish, with eyes wide open, pupils dilated, he gazed at me fixedly. "Bertie," he murmured, "the pain has been bearable, but now it is increasing; if I move in the least the agony is dreadful. Inflammation is beginning I suppose, and if something is not done speedily I must die!"

What could I answer? I expect I looked as dismayed as I felt, for he went on, "But don't grieve, my boy, don't *you* give up; it's a miserable affair, I know, for you as well as for me, but I am not hopeless; no! if you could follow the instructions I can give you I may pull through—I've been thinking it all out."

I was alert instantly. "Everything you tell me

I will do," said I; "your every wish I will carry out. I'm an awful muff at anything like this, you know, yet I'll do my best, and God helping us, we may, as you say, pull through."

At which he told me that some years before he left England he had attended what was called an ambulance class, where instructions were given about "first aid to the injured," and he had been striving to remember all he had learned about broken bones. He told me I must get a strip of wood, smooth and strong, about four feet long, and a number of shorter and thinner pieces for splints.

These I quickly procured. The next things were bandages. We had very little stuff that would answer for them, but our tent, which was of thin duck, would do; so I ripped some of that into strips.

To put the fracture into place was a most difficult task. I hardly dared to handle him, for every touch gave him exquisite pain; yet I had to twist and pull and push until I believed the bones were in the right position. He directed me as best he could, but only at intervals, on account of the torture my unskilled hands were giving him. When, as I hoped, all was as it should be, I placed the splints, each wrapped in the softest stuff I had, close together round the injury; then I wound long bandages over all, tightly and smoothly.

Lastly, outside, from his armpit to his foot, I placed the long strip of wood and bound it to him, round his chest, his middle, and his ankle, fastening it securely and firmly with plenty of bands above and below the fracture.

Meade thanked me when I had finished. He said, with a sad smile, that he believed I had done it as well as if I had been through the course of instructions which he had; then he closed his eyes, exhausted.

He had borne all this with the greatest fortitude, but now a kind of stupor appeared to creep over him. I hoped that it would end in healthy sleep; therefore I quietly made up the fire, lowered the light, and slipped out into the night.

It was absolutely still in the open air, and not so very cold. Not a breath of wind stirred the surrounding foliage; only the ripple of the creek was audible as it flowed tinkling over the stones a few yards from me, and the swish of the water swirling through the sluice.

Patch had come out with me. He was so quiet, so subdued, so sorrowful; it was just wonderful the almost human sagacity of that dog. I had said to him gently as we came out, "We must be very quiet, Patch; you must not bark; your poor master is very ill; we must let him sleep," and the way that dear old fellow looked at me was as if he quite understood what I had said. I believe he did, too, by his actions.

From the hot stuffy cavern, little more than a

burrow, where I had been attending to my poor friend, to the clear air outside, the change was great and most refreshing. I stood beside the creek for some time breathing in the sweet pine-scented air, and thinking very deeply, very seriously.

The sky was cloudless, the stars were gleaming near the southern horizon in great brilliancy, but over the rest of the heavens they were hardly discernible—they were overpowered by the blaze of the Northern Lights. This was no unusual occurrence; rarely when the sky was clear were they absent at night, though on this particular time they were remarkably bright.

I was naturally terribly depressed, wretchedly anxious, all but despairing; yet when I observed this grand display of Almighty power my thoughts rose from these mundane troubles, and I felt that He who marshalled these mysterious forces, whose hand was so plainly visible there, would, if it pleased Him, help us out of this terrible strait, and enable us to bear whatever He chose to send us with patience and trustfulness. I am not ashamed to add that I lifted up my heart in prayer to Him, beseeching Him to be with us.

Certainly I received great relief from this. I took my seat upon an upturned sluice-box, I drew my blanket-coat close round me, for it was freezing, and with dear old Patch beside me, I remained there ruminating for an hour or more.

I could not hide from myself that the position was most serious. I hoped, though I feared, that what I had done for Meade would prove to be successful. I had heard of people fracturing their limbs, and in a few weeks being out and about again as well as ever. But they had skilled attention, whilst we knew nothing about the treatment. I believed that the principal thing was to keep my patient's general health good. I wondered what food I should give him. I ran over the stores we still possessed, and was thankful to remember how much we had, and what a variety. Surely amongst it all I could concoct wholesome and proper things for him.

Then my mind travelled to our work there. I realised that it was all ended for the present, and I fell to wondering how we should ultimately get all our gold away and our gear, for of course there would be no rafting. The creek, the whole country, would be frozen solid and covered deep in snow, long before my poor friend could travel.

It recurred to me next that in the winter, with snow, one could haul heavy loads upon a sleigh, and I believed that we two and Patch could move everything. I actually caught myself planning how I should build one. Indeed it crossed my mind that even if Meade was not strong enough to help drag, that Patch and I could pull him, with our gold too, as far as Dawson City. There, I thought, there might be a doctor, and surely more comfort than in our dismal hole. Women were at Dawson: one whom I had met at that store, it seemed to me, would prove a good friend to us in our need.

As regards our gold, I felt most grateful that we had secured so much, for there would be no lack of means to carry out our needs.

I sat outside thus, thinking of these and many other subjects, until I noticed that the aurora had faded clean away, that the sky in the north-east was crimson, and that ere many minutes another day would have dawned. Then I went inside. Meade was sleeping naturally, breathing gently and regularly, so I lay down myself and slept too.

It was broad day when I awoke. The brilliant sun was scintillating on the ripples of the creek before our doorway. Meade was calling me. "Bertie, dear boy," said he, "I grieve to have awakened you, but oh! I am so thirsty; give me some cold water."

Well, now, I was afraid to do so. I said I must make some hot, open a tin of Swiss milk, and give him that, but he said "No;" that he remembered well when one of his sisters had been ill, she had suffered much because cold water was refused when she craved for it. When the doctor came he gave it her, telling them to remember that at all times it could be given with safety.

On the strength of this I gave Meade what he

longed for, and it did him good. I made him oatmeal porridge; we had a bottle or two of bovril—I gave him some; and really that day he ate so well and was so wonderfully cheerful that I began to believe this would not be such a terribly serious business after all.

The following day, though, his other leg was exceedingly painful: it was sadly cut and bruised. With warm water I washed it. He wished me to apply cold water bandages, but I had, in Ontario, seen so much benefit from using pine gum—which is Venice turpentine, I suppose—for such hurts, that I persuaded him to let me put some on. The gum was oozing from every tree and stump about, wherever we had made a cut with an axe. In a few moments I collected plenty. It was surprising how quickly this stuff gave him relief, and how healing it was.

Meade was in better spirits that evening again. I read to him, we smoked and chatted—he passed a most satisfactory night. Next day he complained much. He said that even the pressure of the blankets on his legs was dreadfully painful.

I easily remedied that: I made a frame of willow twigs to lie over him, to bear off the clothes, which answered well.

"What a kind chap you are, Bertie," said he, after I had done all I could think of for his comfort.

"Kind chap!" I answered smiling. "Suppose it

had been **my leg that** had been broken, what would you have done?—let me lie? And if you had got me in here, you would have neglected me, I suppose, and let things go? **Not** you; you would have done **all** you could for me, my friend. I know that right well, and **so** I'm doing the same **for you,** and intend to—so **say** no more."

As I have said, we were the best of friends, but **the** intimate association this accident occasioned brought us still closer together. I rarely left his side, only for fuel **and other** necessaries. **As for** going on with gold-getting, somehow I could not even think of **it.** I endeavoured **to** keep a **bright** face in my friend's presence, but when alone, or at night when **he** was sleeping, **I had** many terrible fears and uncertainties to ponder about and to **depress me.**

If he did not soon mend! if he got worse! **if he** could not be moved!—these thoughts **were always in** my mind.

The **winter** would **be** upon us directly—it was then the end **of** September—and I knew that we should **be** frozen **in and snowed** up soon, and remain so till **June** of this **year 1897.** Much of the time would be passed **in** darkness; **in** mid-winter there would be but **a** gleam **of** day at noon. These were dismal, unnerving forebodings. I tried to lift my heart **to** whence alone I could expect real help. I sought to repress **all** other thoughts, to just do the best I knew for my friend, and to trust our Heavenly Father for the rest.

To an extent I succeeded, and so many days went by in comparative peace.

We had a terrible gale during this time, I remember: heavy rain and hail accompanied it. The creek rose, it washed away a couple of our sluice-boxes, and seemed as if it would swamp our drive. This roused me to active measures: I piled up rocks and logs in such a way that I secured it against that misfortune.

Meade and I frequently congratulated ourselves about our safety in that dug-out: we knew that nothing short of an earthquake could upset our dwelling. No tents could stand against *that* heavy wind and downpour.

It was dark and dismal enough, surely, but often when we had a bright fire roaring in its corner, the lamp alight, the door tightly closed, and we were lying reading, with Patch curled up between us, we said to each other how thankful we ought to be, and were, I hope, for such comfort in that wild land.

It was during this enforced companionship that my friend opened his mind very freely to me. I don't know if he had any presentiment then of what the end would be—any premonition of still greater trouble ahead. It is impossible to be certain of this, but I have since thought that he had.

He had a very lovable disposition, even when he

was well, and had had to fight with me against wilderness troubles which upset and spoil the temper of most men. When things went wrong ashore or afloat, when our Indians were stupid, when the fates seemed to be dead against us and all appeared to be going wrong, I never remember him becoming really angry, using bad language, or showing anything but the most perfect amiability.

Many will think it is impossible to go through the rough countries of this world, especially such a wilderness as we had traversed, and were then in, or to subdue others' wills to ours, without *showing* a masterful, a domineering spirit. I thought so, and began, when he and I started on this expedition, to assert myself, believing that only thus would we be able to hold our own, or make headway.

Meade, on the contrary, from the first was amiable, friendly, and polite with all—red men and white. I thought this, for a while, unmanly, and feared I should thereby have my hands full of trouble, but I soon found I was much mistaken.

I noticed on board the steamer going up to Juneau, and at Skagway, that the people looked astonished, for a little, at the way in which my friend spoke, his gentleness and consideration to all—never shouting his desires or orders, but asking politely for what he required. Yes, they looked surprised at his uncommon style, for a bit, but were invariably impressed by it; and thinking that he must be a prince, or at least a duke (that was the usual idea), they treated him, as far as they knew, with the same consideration with which he treated them.

And I, as his mate, his friend, came in for the benefit of it.

So, mild and amiable as Meade had been all along, during this sad time he was, if possible, more so. He suffered intensely, I know it now, though at that time I scarcely understood it. Often he could hardly speak for pain and weakness, yet he never neglected to thank me for the slightest thing I did for him, and he never expressed impatience at his sad condition.

Well, that is hardly true; he did frequently bemoan his fate in having brought me to such a pass —that was a great trouble to him.

In vain I begged him not to let that grieve him. I assured him again and again that I had no one dependent on me in England, or anywhere; that my people were well off; that a month or two, or even a year or two, was of no great moment; that even if we had to winter there we should resume work in the spring, and go home with still larger piles in the summer.

He would listen to these remarks, patiently and calmly, but with a smile on his face apparently of unbelief.

Then he would talk gently to me about himself. How he had looked forward with such intense pleasure to going home that fall with plenty, to relieve his loved mother and sisters from all future money worries. He told me a great deal about them, where they lived, and how.

He had been in Australia for two years, and had done some gold-digging there. He had been four years in Canada; like me, he had brought a little money with him, had taken up land in Assiniboia, had struggled there for a couple of years, living wretchedly and prospering not at all, then he had sold all he had, cattle and gear, and had come West.

He took service in the Rockies with the Canadian Pacific Railway at section work, which is, I believe, what is called "plate-laying" in Britain. From there he had gradually drifted to the coast, to Vancouver City, where he had obtained employment on a wharf. There his education helped him, he became a foreman, next he got the post of purser on one of the steamers trading between Puget Sound and the North.

The spring before I met him he was up at St Michael's, in Behring Sea, where he fell in with a man who told him about the gold which was being got away up the Yukon. He had acted on this man's advice, with the result he had already related to me.

He sent his mother a large portion of what he found the year before, told her of his projected expedition with me, and promised that he would "come out" in September, he believed with what would be regarded as a fortune, even in England.

"And now," said he, with a sad sigh, "here I am, laid by the heels—and you too, my friend, on my account—not able even to let them know that I'm alive!"

I did my very best to comfort him. I begged him to have patience, that I hoped before many weeks—when the snow came—that we should get out, "and surely," I added, "from Dawson there is some way of communicating with civilisation."

You understand we really knew very little about the country. We had heard many yarns about the awful winter, and generally had the idea that it would be extremely dismal and melancholy. But we had also been told that with plenty of grub and light and fuel—which we had—people could exist with some little comfort. So we struck the middle opinion, and found it would be bad but bearable.

Well, it was bearable, certainly, or I should not be here; and yet I can aver that the horror of it has not been more than half told yet.

Thank God, we had plenty of food and firing, and as I said to my poor chum, "I'll bet there are many miserable beggars scattered about this Yukon country and Alaska who are worse off than we are by a long shot."

He smiled at my enthusiasm, and added, "But I hope there are no broken legs amongst them."

At which I felt rather subdued. But I had talked, and continued to do so thus, to cheer him if I could, and to make him think that I was quite happy and contented.

Really, at heart, I was neither. He did not seem to me to be improving. He told me of the pain he suffered in his leg. I suggested that it was caused by the bone growing together. I said I had heard that was usually the most painful time, and he hoped I was right. He was very pale and thin. I tried to believe that was only the effect of his lying so long and being in the dim light. His appetite troubled me: he ate very little, and did not fancy anything we had.

One time he talked to me about the girl he loved at home. He showed me her portrait. Her name is Fanny Hume. I thought she must be very pretty from her photo. He declared she was that—lovely. They had been engaged for four years. She was to have come out to him, if he had done well in the prairie country. They had experienced great disappointment at his failure there, but his good fortune up here the year before had altered matters. If he had got out this fall they were to have been married by Christmas.

He told me of the plans he had laid for his mother's comfort, and of the dreams he had about the home he would make for his bride with the good fortune that had come to him. "And now," said he in grievous tones, "all this is ended, all my plans frustrated. God knows how hard it is; it looks almost cruel, doesn't it?"

What could I say? I begged him not to lose hope. I besought him to remember that God *did* know — that for some mysterious reason He had allowed this terrible disaster to take place, that we must just put our trust in Him. We were assured, and, I hoped, believed, that He does all things well, and that we must just leave it so.

Oh! how I longed to have more power of comforting him. How impotent I felt, and was. I could only keep saying, "Look up, Meade! look up! from there alone can come our help."

One day said he, "I'd give anything for a bit of fresh mutton. Just fancy a mutton chop at Pimm's, in the Strand, and a glass of their stout, eh!"

This pleased me. If he had such a longing for food I thought it a good sign, and said so.

But, alas! there was no mutton chop to be got there. There are mountain sheep — bighorns, moufflons — up in the hills. How could I leave him to stalk one? But I thought I might shoot him a grouse for a change. Salmon he was heartily sick of; the tinned things were very good for men in health, but not for an invalid. I had broiled him a bit of bear meat lately, which he enjoyed. I did so again and again, till he was tired of that.

So I took down my gun one day, said I would

not be long away. I thought I would go up and kill a bird.

I went up the creek to a clump of thick spruce I knew of, feeling sure I should find some there, but instead out leapt a half-grown deer!

I brought him down luckily. I could just manage to pack him home. I was back again within an hour. Meade smiled a welcome. "I heard you shoot," said he, "the rifle barrel. What did you get?"

I would not tell him. I said he must wait and see. The little buck was fat. I cut out a chop—it looked just like a mutton chop—I broiled it at a fire I lit outside, and brought it to him. He was delighted, he was charmed, and with tears in his eyes he thanked me again and again. And there were tears in my eyes too!

For several days he enjoyed what he called mutton. I had hung it outside to freeze, where everything was frozen. I varied his food—bear meat, deer meat, salmon; salmon, bear meat, deer meat—and in between I gave him some of the canned things that he fancied.

For weeks matters went on like this. It was five since the accident, when I noticed a decided change in him, and it was not for the better!

It was by that time winter. All green things but the pines and spruces were frozen and dead. Snow covered all the high lands, and even the flats were drifted with it. The still water everywhere was frozen; only our creek still ran, and there were still fish in it. I don't know what possessed me—thank God, something did—but I took the notion to secure some of these salmon.

It was easily done. I rolled a few logs and brush into a narrow place, then went up stream and drove the fish down, and many became entangled there. I dragged out half-a-dozen and slung them in the trees about our den.

Another day I saw a bear foraging about near. I gave Meade warning that I was about to shoot, and I killed it easily. I put a ball through him, under his arm, and he died without a struggle. It was very fat and lazy—a cinnamon.

I had plenty to do to skin it and cut it up. The fat I hung up in the trees. We had no great amount of oil left for our little lamp, and very few candles, and I thought, "If we must winter here we must make shift with this in some way until next June."

For I began to think that my idea of getting out on a sleigh would never work. Yet I was busy constructing one. But I thought I saw that if my friend was to get away it would only be when the water was open again, eight or nine months later!

Our almost finished raft was now frozen fast to the bank. I almost hated the sight of it. I wondered if, after all, that would be the means by which we should get away.

I do not remember that I regarded the prospect of wintering there as such a terrible calamity. We really had plenty about us, and we were such excellent companions that I only felt if he got well, all would be well.

I must admit that it crossed my mind more than once—" If he should die!"

I put this dreadful thought away, I kept it down generally, but sometimes it struck me suddenly, and I felt as if a stream of ice ran down my spine, as though my heart was frozen. The contemplation of such a dire disaster was awful.

Time went on; I could see no improvement. If his leg was joining properly I could not tell, nor could he. He himself was usually very quiet, yet there was a look creeping over him to which I could not shut my eyes; he was thinner, greyer, and shrivelled.

One night he put down his pipe as if with loathing. "I'll smoke no more," said he; "I believe it is not good for me."

I took no notice—thought it better not.

Later he threw down his book, declaring he could not read—that his leg was so painful.

I examined it. So far as I could tell all seemed right—so far as appearance went. His foot was cold and somewhat swollen, but there was warmth enough elsewhere.

Next day he had much more pain. He was all for cold water bandages. To please him I bathed his leg and wrapped it in wet cloths—this eased him.

That night he complained that the half-wet bandages were irritating him. What was I to do?

Finding that cold water applications soothed him, I kept the cloths wet always. Neither of us had the least idea whether we were doing right.

I discovered that he slept very little. I myself passed many a sleepless night, but my health was wonderfully good. I was quite robust in spite of my terrible anxieties.

The weather was now extremely cold—as cold as I had ever felt it in the east of Canada. Our place was warm though—so long as we kept the door closed and excluded draughts we were cosy.

The nights were extremely long, and the days, though usually sunny, were very cold. We had several hard gales: the fine, dry snow was forced through every crevice. I used to bring in abundance of food and fuel at such times, cram every crevice round our doorway full of moss, make Patch come inside, and none of us left the shelter whilst the blizzard lasted.

I had cut a hole in the door and covered it with a piece of the thin intestine of a bear. We had no glass. I used to read to my companion sometimes from a Bible, at others from Shakespeare, and we had a copy of that penny book W. T. Stead has published,

'Hymns that have Helped.' It had got out to Victoria, and I had picked it up at a book-store and valued it, for several of those hymns had powerful associations for me.

My friend was fond of some of them too, and I often saw him read a verse or two with tears in his eyes.

He was generally silent. This made me very sad. Do as I would, try as I did, I could not help being very much cast down, very full of forebodings of evil.

One night—it was bitterly cold outside, and the wind was howling through the trees, we were warm and comfortable enough as far as that went—I was looking sorrowfully at the invalid, who I thought was dozing, when he slowly opened his eyes—which seemed to me to have grown very large and prominent—and gazing at me, oh! so mournfully, said, "Bertie, my friend, I suppose you realise that I am not going to get well?"

For a few moments I could not reply, my heart was in my throat, I felt as if it were choking me; at length I managed to ejaculate, "Oh! Meade, my dear friend, have patience—don't break down like this—or I shall——"

His eyes were suffused with tears. "Dear friend, indeed," he began, slowly and in broken accents, "I grieve—God knows how very much I grieve—to tell you this, but I know I am not improving, and I believe I shall never leave this hut alive. I have been thinking about you, wondering what you will do if I am taken. I am awfully sorry that I brought you here."

"Say not one word on that head," I interrupted him; "*I* do not regret it. Look how well we have done. What has happened is terrible, I know, but oh! pray don't give up, don't get to thinking that you'll not recover. Please God you'll be all right soon, then fancy with what joy we'll be off home in the spring."

Thus I tried to cheer him—thus I tried to look at things.

"Well, well," he replied, with a wan smile, "I'll try to be more hopeful, I'll try to trust; but listen, what will you do if I am taken? Can you make your way out alone, think you?"

I refused to answer,—I merely said that I would not even think about it, much less talk of it, and begged him not to. I asked him if his leg was so painful, and what reason he had to say he was no better, in reply to which he went into a number of particulars which I need not repeat.

Later he talked again about his mother and sisters, and, laying his hand on mine, he begged me to bear with him, not to be angry with him, whilst he explained what he wished to be done, "supposing," and he gazed at me in a most affecting way as he said it,—"supposing I don't get home myself."

I said very little,—I let him talk. I nodded

occasionally to let him see I heard what he was saying, understood, and would do as he wished.

He told me what proportion he desired his mother and his sisters to have—" if I ever got out safely with the gold "—and that the remainder was to be given to Fanny Hume, the lady to whom he was engaged.

He bade me put all these things down in my note-book, saying also that he should write letters to them all, " in case of accidents." He dwelt for some time on these most melancholy topics, and I expect would have gone on still longer had I not diverted his thoughts into another channel.

I got on to the subject of the value of the gold we had, and asked his opinion of the way we were to proceed to secure our claim, so that we might return next season and work it.

He told me again all he knew on the subject, declared that we should have to hire men at Dawson, or at Forty Mile, or even at Circle City, to work for us; and indeed for an hour or two he talked on very much in his old way, full of information and cleverness, and quite excited about the fortune we had made.

He fell asleep at last with a cheerful look on his face, after having by my persuasion smoked a pipe with me.

I rolled myself in my blankets then, and with some hopefulness and a quieter spirit I too went to sleep.

Several times I awoke and put on firing. Meade

was always sleeping peacefully, but towards morning, just as grey light was filtering through our window, I was aroused by his groans. He told me that he was suffering acutely, that the pain in his leg was maddening, that he was sure all had gone wrong there. He begged me to remove the bandages, declaring that he knew they were no longer needed. "Either the bones have joined now, or they never will," said he. "If they have not, then I shall never get better, and if I go on any longer in this agony I shall die surely."

Perplexed, bewildered, terribly afraid of doing wrong, yet quite unable to withstand his entreaties, I consented in the end to do as he desired.

He had already thrown the blankets from him, and was tossing his unhurt leg and arms about most dangerously. His face was flushed, he was continually crying out for water, and I, even with my small experience, knew that he was in a high fever, of the seriousness of which I was conscious.

I loosed the fastenings of the long strip of wood. This did not appease him. He exclaimed that he was on fire, that the pain was excruciating. He became angry with me because I hesitated to take off the splints. He talked wildly, incoherently, madly, and then began tearing at the bandages himself, so I undid the splints and took them off, exposing his bare leg, and then I no longer wondered that he suffered as he did.

He fainted, I believe, and when the pressure was

taken off he lay back pale and silent. I brought whisky, and by degrees got him to swallow some. I opened the door, brought in some snow, which covered everything outside now. I put some on his forehead. He was a long time, or so it seemed to me, before he came to.

I cannot describe the appearance of his leg; it horrified me. From that moment I gave up all hope of his recovery. It was indeed some time before he spoke, and then he was delirious, light-headed. He talked and raved the whole night through. Sometimes he begged me to remove the bandages—which were off; at others he talked of his mother, of Fanny Hume, often of Jim and Fan, and of me and of our work. I never went through such a day and night—I never want to again. Towards morning he fell asleep, exhausted. I wondered if I had done wisely in removing these bandages. I thought not. He slept now so profoundly that I endeavoured to replace some of them without awaking him, and I did succeed in getting the long strip down his side and securing it just as he awoke. He was in his right mind then, and I believe had no knowledge of the condition he had been in.

He endeavoured to move his leg—he could not. I suppose he recognised the importance of this discovery, for he then threw himself back, extended his arms, and sighed profoundly as he muttered, "It is so, then—the case is hopeless! hopeless!"

He looked at me once, a fixed solemn look, then closed his eyes and lay there motionless and silent.

I whispered, "Oh! try, dear friend, not to move that leg, the only hope is to keep it absolutely still." Then he opened his eyes, gazed at me for a moment, and through his clenched teeth he whispered, "Hopeless, hopeless."

The rest of that day he was profoundly quiet. I don't think he slept, for whenever I spoke to him he replied at once in a monosyllable. He would not eat, but drank all I gave him.

I myself was so low and exhausted with anxiety and watching that I have but little recollection of what followed. Sometimes he slept, sometimes his mind wandered, generally he was in a state of stupor. One morning I left him sleeping whilst I went out for food and fuel. When I returned, to my horror he was sitting upright.

I called out in amazement. He smiled sadly as he said, "Ah! it does not matter much, Bertie. I've not moved my bad leg though, just dragged it along —it's all right, as right as it'll ever be: but I must write to-day; after that we'll just hope for the best, that's all we can do."

"Ay," I answered, "that's all; yes, but we can pray, we can do that, and that's our only hope."

He begged me to give him paper and pencil, and for an hour or more he wrote. He stopped often to sip the drink I set beside him, then he lay back exhausted, and I think he slept.

By-and-by he aroused and wrote more letters. He went on thus until it was quite dark, when he told me he had finished, adding that he believed he now could sleep well, for a great weight was off his mind.

Before he closed his eyes I begged him to tell me if there was anything I could do for him, any wish that I could gratify. Would he have bovril? whisky? tea? He thanked me; he said he had no desire for anything, that he would sleep; but suddenly opening his eyes, looking at me excitedly, he said, "Bertie, you will not laugh at me, you will not think I'm off my head, will you, but if you'd just read me that beautiful hymn of Cowper's — "There is a fountain," you know? I remember it was a a great favourite of Prince Albert's, and I like it too. Read it for me, Bertie, and then I think I'll sleep well."

I read it—I broke down several times—but as I finished the last line I saw he was sleeping calmly.

I was fagged out myself—I had hardly eaten a scrap that day—I don't think I had slept an hour for days; so when I saw he was sleeping I too lay back and was soon unconscious, and had forgotten all our troubles.

Before closing my eyes though, I took a good look at my friend. I could not help remarking how great a change there was in him. His face was so drawn, so withered; there was no trace of colour on it, even his lips were white.

I had never seen a human being die. I had never seen a dead person up to that time, and yet there was that appearance to my companion; something had come over him which profoundly affected me, and I kept saying to myself, "He will die, he will die." I was whispering this when I fell asleep, and forgot all my grief and misery.

How long I slept I do not know. It was still dark when I awoke. I had extinguished the light before I went to sleep. It was very cold, the fire was nearly out. This being an all-important affair I jumped up, stirred the embers together and blew them into a flame. Then I piled on more wood, and made quite a noise in doing it.

I feared I had awakened Meade and perhaps alarmed him. I called gently to him. There was no reply. I concluded that he still slept, therefore I crouched by the now blazing fire, warming myself.

Just then Patch came quietly up to me and laid his head on my arm. I looked down and patted him.

Really and truly there was a most pitiful look in the poor dog's eyes. He saw that I noticed this, and to my horror and dismay he suddenly lifted up his head and gave one most vehemently long-drawn, heartrending howl!

Speaking sharply to the poor beast, I clasped his

muzzle, and he stopped. Then he sat staring at the blazing logs with a most sorrowful expression.

I don't know why, I can't tell what made me begin to tremble. I reached for a lighted sliver—I could hardly hold my hand still enough to light the lamp, I shook so—and when I had ignited it and turned it on to the face of my friend, I saw that he had not moved since he fell asleep. There he lay, stretched out on his back, sleeping still. Yes, surely, he was sleeping!

Softly I laid my hand on his forehead—it was cold as ice. I sought for one of his hands—it was cold and as stiff as if it were frozen. I put my hand upon his heart—there was no motion there.

Then like a flash it came to me that my dear friend was dead—ay, Meade was dead!

CHAPTER VI.

It is impossible to tell you what I felt when I realised that my friend had breathed his last.

I cannot myself remember what my thoughts and sensations were. I only know that I rushed out of the place—very lightly clothed, too—and in the open air stood gazing around me dazed.

The first few hours after that is nearly a blank to me. I can merely call to mind cold, hunger, snow, and poor Patch's evident distress. I made a fire outside and we sat by it, I repeating to myself, sometimes crying aloud, "What shall I do? What shall I do?"

Once I remember springing up and grasping a white shirt and a red one which lay by the door, and tying them to a long branch which arched across the creek conspicuously, saying to myself, "It may attract some one's notice,"—for, eager as we had been all along to keep our presence secret, now I would gladly have given half, ay, all the gold we had obtained, to secure the companionship of a human being.

The days were very short then. There was but a gleam of sunlight at noon, and as this faded to the south behind an ice-clad mountain, a strong breeze arose which roared through the tree-tops. There was a wildness and weirdness about its dirge-like roar which seemed to me quite in keeping with what had happened.

I had taken no food all day. I had not been inside the hut. I could not for long muster courage to enter it. To gaze upon my lost friend's features seemed impossible — the idea of stopping for any time in the same place with his poor body was beyond me, yet I knew I must do something. Food at least I must procure for myself and Patch; if we had this I believed that we could exist beside the huge fire I had built until I grew calmer, and could decide on some course of action. I put off doing anything though as long as possible, and not until it was quite dark did I creep into our dismal abode.

I trod gently, with awe, for I could not divest myself of the idea that poor Meade could hear me, that my dear friend was at least present in spirit. But truly I cannot tell what I thought or what I felt.

The fire was out. I lit the lamp. I gazed fearfully around—avoiding the face, white and drawn, which I knew was amongst the pile of bedding there. Why was this? Why does one naturally dread to look upon a dead face? Surely I had got to love my friend, and to know that he loved me. There was no reason for this unwillingness to look, but so it was then, and so it usually is.

I threw a blanket over his poor body, snatched a rug up, a loaf of bread, a piece of cooked venison, some tea and sugar, and hastened out again, closing the door securely.

It was blowing harder now; fine snow was being whirled through the forest and down the creek, which had long since ceased to flow. It was freezing very hard; everything was ice-bound; my fire gave but little warmth. What could I do?

Really I was so utterly cast down, so despairing, that I was reckless. It seemed to me just then that nothing mattered, and that I too should soon die, and lie as Meade did, until perhaps long afterwards some wandering prospector would find our bones, our gold, and our belongings; but our real story, or who we were, would never be known.

Patch ate the food I gave him, and I managed to swallow something: then we crouched, he and I, with the rug round us. He slept, but I was thinking—thinking.

The cold increased, the bitter wind was piercing. I roused myself to pile on fuel. A gust of exceeding sharpness seemed to shrivel me, and it flashed through me that another such blast would end me.

For a second I thought, "So much the better"; but at the same moment, like a vision, there passed across my half-benumbed consciousness a picture of what my dear dead friend had told me about his mother and his sisters, and the dearest one of all. I knew what he had said about the benefit the gold that we had found would be to them, and how I had promised him to fight hard to get it to them should he not recover.

My own future did not trouble me. I had no one dependent on me, but I suddenly felt strong in what I saw was my bounden duty. I straightened myself up and exclaimed, "No; I'll not give in! I'll fight this matter through, God helping me!"

I must have spoken loudly, and I suppose cheerily, for Patch jumped from his nook beside the fire, looked at me brightly, eagerly, waved his grand tail, and made me think that he had understood my exclamation, approved it, and would gladly aid me.

The bitter wind blew keenly past us, the powdery snow penetrated every crevice in my clothing, my beard was a mass of ice, and I knew that a few minutes more of this terrible cold would be fatal.

Still I could not bring my mind to going into that dismal den again, or to remain there with the body of my friend beside me.

How should I proceed then? I thought hard. If I could only get shelter from this awful blizzard, I believed I could manage to exist until I could plan something. But where was there shelter! I gazed around; there was no bank, no rock, nothing which offered the slightest protection from the furious blasts.

Something must be done, however—to stay where I was meant death. The very fire was being blown away and smothered in the snow-drifts.

Just then the tunnel we had excavated occurred to me. I grasped a glowing firebrand, gathered a bunch of sticks, and rushed to the entrance, Patch excitedly following me. Pushing my way over the obstructions I had placed there as protection from the flooded creek, I entered, passed in a dozen feet, and found this retreat was dry enough, and such a good protection from the wind and snow outside that it felt quite warm. I flung down my fire-stick and soon had a blaze, gladly perceiving that the smoke ascended to the roof and passed out, leaving a clear space below where we could sit or lie without annoyance.

I was so pleased with this arrangement that I made excursions for fuel, and actually went into the shanty for my blankets, more food, a kettle, and a lamp.

And in this retreat Patch and I remained some days, I only venturing out for firewood, of which, most happily, I had a good heap cut.

The storm raged furiously and ceaselessly, the snow fell continuously, it all but closed the entrance to the tunnel; but having a pick and shovel, I was able to keep an opening for air and to let out the smoke.

Patch and I lay there warm and snug enough. It was, however, a most dismal experience—worse even than that Nansen endured on his famous expedition towards the Pole, for he had companionship. I had none.

I tried hard to pull myself together, to make some sort of programme for future action, but I could do very little — the power of consecutive thought seemed to have left me. I passed the time eating, smoking, sleeping—it was to me like some dreadful dream, and I often, often caught myself wondering when I should awake, and the misery would be over.

I suppose it was then the end of November, and I knew there would be no real spring, no open water, till June; seven months of this desolation and loneliness to look forward to! for I had come to the resolve that, in any event, so long as provisions held out, even for months, or years, I would not abandon the gold.

I had calculated, and I knew perfectly well, that Patch and I together could not haul it out on a sled, with what we must take of gear and food. No; we must stay there till spring, and what I could, or would, do then I did not settle: I only had a vague idea that I would pack everything on the all but finished raft, and somehow float it down to Dawson.

I had plenty of time to plan all this, I knew. At intervals my memory dwelt on what now seemed to me to have been the real comfort, the real content, which Meade and I had experienced in that miserable dug-out before his accident. My mind reverted to the pleasant evenings he and I had passed with books and pipes, anticipating the joys that were in store for us when we had got out, and had once more set foot upon dear English soil. How we used to talk, and plan, and prophesy! Alas! all was ended, his career had been cut short, as we have seen, and mine—well, I did not think about mine very much, the present was what troubled me: the awful loneliness, the misery of it, was what occupied me.

I was forced to go into the den occasionally for necessaries. I had not removed the covering from my friend's face, but I had grown a little bit familiar with that melancholy heap of bedding, and the fact that he lay there, frozen, did not now so greatly agitate me.

The storm raged ceaselessly for quite a week, then suddenly there was perfect silence outside. I went forth to investigate; whether it was day or night I could not tell, for there was but little sunrise really then—the stars were gleaming in a cloudless sky. It was absolutely calm, so the cold was bearable, yet I knew it was more intense than I had ever before felt it.

The moon was rising, and a wonderful scene it was that her beams shone on; beautiful, I have no doubt, but to me then, and always, it was most awful desolation.

Everything—our workings, the raft, the creek—was covered deeply with snow; I could barely make out the door of the dug-out. I looked at it very sorrowfully, and I wished—I was almost ashamed of that wish, I thought it desecration—that I dare go in and live there, even with the companionship of all that remained of my dear friend.

I brought the shovel, removed the snow, and as I was doing so it came to my mind that if I were only able to bury Meade's body I could return to the den and pass the winter there.

But where could I bury it? How could I dig a grave? Everything, I knew, was frozen hard as steel; should I clear away the frozen nigger grass and moss, and light a fire on the earth in some quiet nook, thaw it thus, and dig a grave, as miners sink their holes in winter?

I returned to my fire in the tunnel to think this out. How terrible it all appeared in there; how I longed to make the change! I sat pondering on this for some little time, and then I had an idea.

I grasped a pick and drove it into the wall of the drive behind the fire, and found that I could excavate the earth easily. I went to work, for I had determined what to do.

Soon I had cut a niche quite large enough to hold the body. I smoothed it nicely, procured some fresh pine twigs which I strewed in it; then going to the shanty, I forced myself to draw the dear fellow's remains, upon the same bear-skin he had passed away on, to the sepulchre that I had hewed.

The body was frozen, of course, and was as easily handled as if it had been a log of wood. I took everything from his pockets, then I rolled it into its resting-place—a temporary one I regarded it. I strewed spruce branches over it, and covered it reverently with the earth I had removed, and soon no one but I could have told that a brave young Englishman, a loved friend, a dear companion, was sleeping his last sleep in there. I smoothed the opening over, but I knew right well the spot where Percy Meade, my lost friend, was lying entombed.

It was done at last, the mournful task was ended; having the Prayer-book with me, I read with tear-dimmed eyes some passages aloud from it — good Patch sitting by as quiet and sedate as if he understood it all.

There was no hurry, no need for haste, and yet as soon as this sad business was finished I left the tunnel gladly, and entered the shanty with the lamp.

It was awfully cold in there—it was an ice-house; but I soon had a fire blazing in the corner. I piled on logs, and on them heaped the withered pine brush and rubbish with which the floor had been strewed. Then I cut fresh stuff, brought in the bear and deer-skins, the rugs and blankets I had been using in the tunnel, heaped them before the fire to dry, and in a few hours I was, so far as bodily requirements went, in comfort.

As I gazed around me then, I was very sad. On the rough shelves we had constructed were lying the few books and papers we possessed, and there were some odds and ends which poor Meade had greatly valued. There was his pipe and tobacco-box, his plate and knife and fork, which he had been so fastidious about—two or three photographs of home scenes and a portrait or two were pinned to the logs about the dismal shanty.

All these had been the texts of many a long yarn, many an interesting conversation—it was very sad. But I did not remove them; there seemed to me a sacredness about them, a melancholy sort of interest which was my only comfort in that dismal cave. They brought back to me many and many an incident, and were to some extent a kind of companionship to me in my loneliness. However, I was very weary with all this unaccustomed grievous labour. I made tea, cooked some food, then putting a huge log on the fire, which I knew would last for hours, I fell asleep and dreamt. I thought that I was far away from all these horrors, back in my dear old home, with loving faces round me, my troubles over, my long agony past, and all forgotten. Oh, blessed, thrice blessed sleep!—thank God for sleep!

It was a long time since either of us had written a word in our diary. I was not at all certain of the day, much less of the hour, when Meade had died. I spent some time trying to puzzle this out, endeavouring to account for the time that had elapsed since Meade left me, and, so far as I could guess, for day and night were very much the same then, and had been for weeks, it was ten days—but I had nothing to guide me with certainty. However, I assumed that it was on the 8th November that he died, and I determined to start my watch again, and during every twenty-four hours that passed henceforth to make some entry in our book, and this I am glad now that I adhered to.

Our gold was buried in a corner of the den; I had lost interest in it. Occasionally the thought came to me that it was there all right; but as to looking at it, or adding to it, that never crossed my mind. All my thoughts then were how to get away from the dreadful place. I had come to the opinion that if I left that gold behind me it would be secure enough, for I imagined that I was alone in an entirely unknown country, and that if I left it, it would remain unknown for many a year.

So I thought and thought continually on this one subject—how to get out. I read a little, ate more, smoked much, slept half my time, and thus the hours went slowly by until I fancied it was

I

Christmas Day, and still I had arranged no definite plan.

I had got into an exceedingly low, stupid, almost imbecile condition. I had no heart, no energy for anything; I seemed to have no "go" left in me. I suppose the continual darkness, the utter loneliness, was telling on me. I look back now and wonder at my state: I, who had always been hitherto full of vigour, resourceful, hardly ever despondent, and hating to be idle for a moment, was leading a purely animal life, just eating and sleeping, with very little power, seemingly, of even thinking of the future.

It was then, as I supposed, Christmas Day; anyway, it was a very calm and quiet day. The northern lights were brilliant, and Patch and I were outside: I was gathering fuel and cutting some logs for the fire, he was rolling in the dry dust-like snow, and sniffing at the meat and salmon which hung frozen in the trees around us. I looked about at the brilliant scene, I gazed aloft in adoration at the wonderful display. I felt awed and solemnised at what I saw, and the question came to me, seemed to hit me almost like a blow—"Was I doing wisely, manfully? was I doing my duty to myself, or carrying out faithfully the promises I had made to Meade?" Again in fancy I saw his mother and his other dear ones in some quiet, rural, English home, such as he had described to me, longing for news of him and his fortunes; perhaps suffering for the want of the money he had promised them so surely, that money which was now lying useless in the corner of the shanty.

Could I not do something even then? I asked myself. Must six more melancholy months drag their slow length along? Must I wait for the opening of the water in June? Could I not take even a few pounds' weight of gold, food, furs, and blankets on a sled, and somehow get down to Dawson, where I knew that there were people, and where I could but fancy there must be some means of communicating with the outer world?

Such thoughts as these crowded through my brain. I seemed suddenly to awaken to my responsibilities.

I knew it was but a hundred miles at most to Dawson City; so surely Patch and I could manage to do that—and as anything was better than going on as I had been of late, I determined to adventure.

I had not been twenty yards from the hut or tunnel for weeks; but then, I at once waded out to the middle of the creek. It was more than wading. The light snow was up to my waist, and I plainly saw that I could not make headway through it, and that it would be utterly impossible to draw a loaded sleigh over it. The dryness of the atmosphere and the intense cold had not allowed the snow to pack.

If I had snow-shoes, I wondered if I could manage

to move about. But I had none. However I had a few flour-barrel hoops of ash. I bent a couple somewhat into the shape of snow-shoes, roughly netted some cord across them, and essayed to use them, and found they answered the purpose sufficiently to encourage me first of all to make as good a pair as possible.

I set eagerly to work. I bound hoops together closely and braced them; I cut bearskin into strips, well twisted them, laced them across and across as well as I could remember they were laced in proper ones; I used some wire we had to strengthen them; and in the course of some days' close labour I had constructed a pair of very rough but, as I soon proved, serviceable snow-shoes.

With these I practised walking. Most days Patch and I took tramps up and down the creek, and I very soon became dexterous in their use: besides, I knew it was necessary for me to take plenty of exercise to knit myself together, to train for my contemplated expedition.

Now I turned my attention to the construction of a sled—a sledge. The one I had begun I had not seen for weeks,—it was buried under many a foot of snow. I searched, and at last dug it out; it was, I could see, unsuitable. I realised that I must make a sort of toboggan—something to lie flat upon the snow, that would not cut into it as sled-runners would.

No wood suitable for this purpose grew about there. I passed many hours in the bright moonlight, searching the immediate neighbourhood; but they were all rough trees, and would not answer. I was perplexed, puzzled, till I thought of the sluice-boxes, and on one of them I set to work, and with the few tools I had I managed to make what I felt sure would do. But every day or night Patch and I took marches up and down the creek; sometimes these trips extended for miles.

I knew too that I must carry with me some sort of arrangement for sleeping in, and contrive a portable shelter, as I had torn up the little tent for bandages for Meade. The former—the sleeping-bag —I made of what remained of the bear-skins, to which I joined deer-skins, and I lined it with fox, silver-grey and black, of which I had quite a number. The tent I made up of what remained, with some blankets and such materials. I had already contrived additional warm clothing of fur and blankets, with a hood or capote.

With all this business the days passed quickly and, may I say, hopefully.

Just then a great need assailed me. I had run out of lamp oil, and the candles had long since been used up. I tried to work by firelight, but that was very difficult. Then I bethought me of the lumps of bear fat hanging in the trees, and I brought some in, and with an empty meat tin and a piece of rag I made a very successful lamp, and that difficulty was surmounted.

My sled, or toboggan, was ready. My snow-shoes answered well. I had made alterations and improvements in them as I had gained experience, and I was now able to get about on them with speed and comfort.

It was towards the end of January, according to my calculations, and I began to reckon eagerly of making a start.

The wretchedness, the inexpressible loneliness of this time, was really awful. At times I was half beside myself with horror, and I suppose I acted like a half-crazed being often. I used to talk to Patch, to address him as if he were a human being, and the dear old dog would put his head on one side, prick up his ears and listen to me, and I do believe he tried his best to understand what I said to him. What I should have done without that dear old fellow I cannot imagine.

One day—or night, was it?—Patch and I were up the creek some miles. I had my gun with me, for I had the day before noticed traces of what I thought were wolves, and I did not care to be confronted with them unprepared.

I was standing in an open space, clear of trees, on the surface of the frozen stream indeed, when I was more than usually struck with the sublime, the awful spectacle which the heavens exhibited.

These magnificent displays of the aurora borealis always affected me; but this night they were particularly grand, and I stood some time, as there was not a breath of wind stirring, admiring them, and wondering.

Streamers, tongues of rose-tinted lurid fire, slowly crept up from the mysterious north. Sometimes they stopped, hesitated, then darting on again, covered the entire heavens. Often they resembled huge flames of crimson fire; they flickered and seemed often to be enshrouded in dense, yet transparent, smoke. Frequently they whirled and twirled as if they had been spindles.

Now these appearances were here, now there. They never remained stationary; the whole firmament was in motion always.

The snow and all the earth and trees were bloodcoloured, my breath and the dog's was red too, and awful. There was a certain feeling of suffocation in the atmosphere, or so I imagined. The cold was indescribable; inhaling felt like drawing into one's throat the fumes of cayenne pepper. My heart beat violently, I breathed in gasps, and I knew that if a wind arose I should be shrivelled up as feathers would be in a fire.

But I also knew that Providence had decreed that when cold has become so intense, as it was then, wind shall not blow; therefore, I dismissed this dread.

At times the heavens were suffused with deepest

crimson, then bars of glowing scarlet would undulate across them; or it would be checkered with different tints of orange purple and deep green.

And suddenly all these colours vanished, and the sky was covered with what looked like luminous clouds, through which moved shapes of wavy light, forms which could be likened to angels or spirits. They arose from the northern horizon, climbed slowly to the zenith, then with a burst of brilliance they slipped out of sight. It seemed to me that hundreds, thousands of them were up there moving, twining, turning amongst themselves, like sentient beings, through all the vast space above me.

These forms, wrapped in robes of diaphanous, tremulous light, sometimes appeared as if they were about to leave the sky and wrap me about in fleecy raiment, and I caught myself imagining that they would carry me away beyond those snow-clad mountains to the north, to the spot which all men seek, but which none have yet reached. I was spellbound, dazzled by this sublime exhibition of Almighty power. I was not afraid—not really; I was awestruck, solemnised.

And as this wonderful white light poured over the pine-clad hills and flashed on the ice-clad mountains, and the nearer trees were fringed with silvery glow, and as I watched all this, entranced, I perceived that this splendour was by degrees dying from the sky. The brilliant lights were fading slowly, and in their place the full moon wheeled up, the stars became visible, and it was an ordinary moonlight scene; but so bright, so brilliant, that for a while I was unable to decide which was the more wonderful display, this calm and peaceful scene, or that which had but now faded from the heavens leaving no trace behind.

I had not stirred for quite half-an-hour, and Patch had stood by me, motionless, all the time. Strangely —or so it was to me—he did not appear to have noticed any of these lights and sights. He was perfectly impassive.

I had thought during the height of this spectacle that I heard cracklings and other noises like electric discharges; but now that all was motionless about me and no aurora visible, I still heard these sounds, and decided that they were caused by the intense frost splitting trees and splintering their bark and branches.

I was about to turn towards home—home! fancy speaking of that dreadful place I stayed in as home! —when I heard a sound far to the east, beyond some hills, which struck me as most strange. It was exactly like the discharge of a double-barrelled gun.

I noticed that Patch pricked up his ears at it, and looked suddenly alert.

I listened intently for some minutes, then I heard that sound again!

It was the frost at work, I reckoned, and yet there was something about the report that excited me. I waited, listening for some time, but as I did not hear the sound again, Patch and I wandered back to fire and food.

However, these peculiar sounds frequently recurred to me. There was a strange persistency in my thoughts about them. I wondered if it was possible that some people were stopping over the hills, or could it be merely the snapping of the frost. I concluded that this latter was the solution, and fell asleep believing so.

CHAPTER VII.

THE following day—I call it day, because my watch indicated eight in the morning—I went to work, determined to lose no time in finishing all I had to do before starting. There was a collar and traces to make for Patch, and a few other things to complete. I stuck to this employment till evening, when it blew hard, snow fell in flurries, and it was again a blizzard. This lasted for two entire days.

Every few minutes during this time my thoughts reverted to that sound which had attracted me up the creek. I could not get rid of the notion that some people might be there. I tried to look the matter squarely in the face, endeavouring to convince myself that even if it were so, it was of no consequence to me.

I was going down stream; I was ready to leave; in a couple more days, if the weather settled, I should be off, and would, I trusted and believed, quickly arrive at where people dwelt. I knew the way. I could not miss the way. How much better for me this was than setting out on an indefinite hunt into a region still farther from the haunts of men.

Thus I reasoned, thus I endeavoured to pacify my thoughts, but again and again there came over my spirit the fancy that there might be some one, not so many miles off, who was as much in need of companionship, who was just as lonely as I was. I cannot explain why I felt thus. I had merely heard, repeated twice, two cracks that sounded like gunshots, that was all, whilst the woods and the ice on which I had stood were full of similar noises.

It was, I suppose, the great desire, the mighty longing that I had for the company of a fellow-being that thus agitated me.

This seemed to me to be the greatest pain I suffered; it was indeed my chief longing to meet a human being—white, black, or red. Just then I believe I should have hailed enthusiastically the poorest specimen of an Indian, the meanest white man in all the country.

Meade had only been gone about eleven weeks, it is true, although it appeared to me that I had been eleven years alone.

On the third evening, which was intensely, indescribably cold, but calm and clear, with brilliant moonlight—stimulated by these thoughts and anxious for action, I started off with my good dog, determined, if possible, to satisfy my longing. I meant, if necessary, to go farther up the creek than I had yet been, up a branch of it which appeared to trend in the direction in which I had been attracted by the peculiar sounds.

I put half a loaf of bread into my bag, some meat, a lump of chocolate, and a pot to boil water in. For a wonder I did this—I rarely took any food with me, but this time it occurred to me as possible that I might have to be out some time—and, as you will learn, it was indeed providential that I did.

Patch and I marched off along the wide avenue which our stream formed through the scrubby firs and Jack pines which grew closely along its margins. We halted first at the place where we had stopped previously, and listened again.

There were the frost-sounds frequent enough, but nothing more. We halted there some little time; Patch was not interested, he sat beside me listless. Then we trudged on a piece farther up the arm, which pointed, as nearly as I could guess, south-west, and this was towards where I thought that I had heard the shots. Here the stream had spread out some width, there was a wide expanse of unruffled snow, and the sounds made by the frost were nearly inaudible.

We waited there again, and to my surprise and amusement Patch became quite animated. He stood beside me, gazing solemnly ahead, with his tail waving slowly, his ears pricked up. He seemed to be listening, as I was, very intently. We stood some minutes thus. I was very cold, but I spoke cheerily to Patch.

He paid no attention to me, just gazed wistfully before him. Yet no sound like a gunshot broke the silence.

I had become impatient; with my mittened hand I patted my companion's head, saying something to him about the futility of this—that it was all hallucination, imagination—at which he looked at me for a moment gravely, then pointed his nose upstream once more, and with his ears erect listened again.

But I could not stand still any longer. I spoke to Patch about it. He paid no attention, at which I turned, meaning to retrace my steps.

I saw he was unwilling to go with me; indeed he sat down in the snow and pointed his nose persistently up the creek, at which it occurred to me we might just as well go on a little farther, as I knew we could not lose ourselves, and I knew, alas! that there was no one "at home" to be troubled about our absence, so I turned again, crying, "Come, my lad! come on, then!"

At this the good old dog began to wag his tail, to jump and caper around me, barking with delight. I had not seen him so excited for weeks, not even when he thought he had a fox cornered, or a rabbit entangled in a snow-drift.

Often he stood still suddenly, as if he had heard something deeply interesting, and always after these intermissions he went ahead with greater demonstrations of pleasure and excitement, which caused me to become more agitated: I wondered what his meaning was.

After a while, when we were standing side by side, attentive, suddenly the stillness, which was oppressive, was broken by two shots!

No doubt of it this time, they were shots! and not so very far away.

Patch looked at me delighted. I am sure he was. Instinctively I took him by the collar, for I thought he might in his transports rush off and get into mischief.

However, a very few minutes after the sound of the shots had ceased to echo amongst the hills, six cracks rang through the stillness. It was a revolver that had been fired, that was sure!

I loosed the dog then, who rushed off in the direction of the sound, whilst I floundered after him, calling as I ran, "Forward, good dog! Forward!"

We must have gone half a mile before we stopped again to listen. Patch had been running ahead barking, then returning to me, showing his eagerness, his delight, urging me with all his powers to hurry on.

But I was out of breath. I stood still, and then I heard a double shot fired once more, and six revolver shots immediately after, and they were much nearer than the last!

There was no mistake about it then. There were other human beings in that awful wilderness, there were more folk suffering—perhaps as I was—for I could not help regarding these reports as signals, perhaps signals of distress.

I thought it well now to make a response. I raised my gun, let fly both barrels, then I drew my revolver from its case and discharged, at regular intervals, all six cartridges, saying, as I did so, "We'll try what that will do, Patch."

Very little time elapsed before I had my answer. The signal was repeated.

It may be imagined what I felt. The knowledge that there was really some person there was pleasing; it was also extremely agitating. I rejoiced that I should soon greet a fellow-creature; that I was not alone in that vast region, in that wilderness of snow and ice. This knowledge was quite overpowering— for a few seconds I could neither speak nor move.

Quickly, however, recovering some composure, I hurried on after Patch, who was rushing ahead and barking vehemently.

Those shots had seemingly been fired on the far side of a low bare hill, which I hurried up, cheering on the dog, making my way with all the speed I could to the summit of the ridge. Fortunately I had the presence of mind to note the course I must take to return to our creek.

This hill was steeper than it looked to be; it took

me some time to mount it, and when at last I stood upon its top I saw no sign of life, nothing but the vast snow-fields, sprinkled here and there with black pines.

Here I fired again, Patch all the time barking exuberantly, and I, feeling sure that I was on the point of some wonderful discovery, felt very strange.

As I stood panting with the exertion of my climb through that chill dry air, I wondered what I could possibly expect to find in those terrific wilds—rough miners, possibly Indians, more likely some one as unfortunate as myself, that was all.

However, the response to my signal was not delayed; down in the valley below there was what appeared to be a door thrown open. A flood of light shone forth, and in the glare of it there stood a figure, whether man or woman, friend or foe, I did not stay to consider—I just bowed my head in thankfulness. This person discharged a double-barrelled gun, then, running out, brandished a blazing firebrand to attract attention evidently, at which I started forward.

I soon had to stop, out of breath, and then I heard the outcry of a human being, and what was most astonishing, it seemed to be the voice of a woman in distress.

Patch had already disappeared. I hastened after him, but had to halt again: the declivity was very steep, the way was encumbered with fallen timber and scrub, it was difficult to descend; so what with

K

the thin cold air and my hurry, I made slow progress, and had to rest frequently.

At one of these rests I saw against the light of the open door my dog crouched at the feet of the person there, who was stooping to caress him.

I hurried on again, and soon could understand what the woman cried; it was, "Help! oh, help! White man or Indian, come and help us!"

I shouted in reply—the distance was very short between us now—"I'm English! You may trust me! I'll come to you as speedily as possible!"

And, as I began to flounder on again, I heard her exclaim most eagerly, "Thank God! Thank God!"

It was not long after this before I reached her and the dog. As I approached she stood up and gazed at me.

She was so enveloped in rugs and clothing that it was impossible to make out from her figure what she was; only two piercing eyes were visible, intently fixed on me. We stood thus, looking at each other for several seconds, then she exclaimed, "Oh! I'm so grateful that you're an Englishman! I'm sure you'll help me if you can."

Her voice thrilled me; I knew instinctively that she was a young woman; moreover, her tone, her accent, assured me that she was no rough and common one. Was I in a dream? I could not realise what had come to pass; I merely said, "Most certainly, I'll help you; what is the matter?"

Then she begged me to come inside the dwelling: I followed her, Patch entering with us. Shutting the door closely, and drawing a curtain across it, she pointed to a rough stool, asked me to remove my snow-shoes and be seated.

I glanced around; I was in a fair-sized log shanty, one end of which appeared to be the fireplace, which, being piled up with blazing logs, filled the low room with light and most welcome warmth. There were two nooks curtained off with coloured blankets. Behind one of them my conductress disappeared, but only for a few moments, when she appeared again. I was greatly embarrassed, for she had removed her wraps, and stood before me a tall and graceful girl, who impressed me instantly with the feeling that I was in the presence of a saint, for the glow from the fire, shining on her fair hair, which was in disorder round her head, formed a halo, an aureole.

Her face, indeed, was thin, drawn, and bore a most distressed expression, but for all that my first glance showed me that it was a beautiful, a supremely beautiful, girl in whose presence I stood.

When I had removed my capote and outer clothing, she glanced at me, and I noticed she gave a sigh of relief when she saw that I was a young man—rough, unkempt, and anything but clean, certainly—but not a ruffianly bushman, as she no doubt had feared I would prove to be; then sitting down by her fire,

I asked, "Now, what can I do to help you? What is wrong?"

She looked at me very sorrowfully, tears filled her eyes, she sobbed, she strove to reply to me; it took same time for her to attain the power of speech, whilst I regarded her with extreme interest and sympathy. At length she murmured, "I am not alone here—my father is lying in there," and she pointed to the other curtained place. "He is lying there very ill—dying, I'm afraid; it is for him that I want help."

I told her that I was greatly grieved for her, but that, unfortunately, I knew little or nothing about illness. I asked if there were no others camped about there—were they entirely alone?

She assured me that, so far as they knew, there was no human being within a hundred miles of them, and that the great trouble was, they had no food, —that they were actually starving!

"Do you mean," I asked, horrified, "that you really have nothing here to eat? How long have you been like this?"

She told me that for weeks they had had nothing but salmon and a little tea; no bread, no meat—nothing but what she had mentioned. "And for a sick man," she went on, "what are they? I have tried to cook this fish in various ways, to get him to eat, but it is useless; he has had nothing but tea for many days—he's dying of starvation!"

"And you," I said; "how have you managed? Have you had nothing but salmon?"

She replied reluctantly, "Oh, I've done well enough. I can eat the fish, and have done so all the time; but now, alas! that too is consumed! We are just perishing for want of food—it is dreadful. What am I to do? Can *you* help us?"

I was unbuckling my bag now. "Come," said I; "cheer up, then. If that is all that's wrong, I can soon make it right;" and when I put the piece of bread and meat upon the rough table, and unfolded the cake of chocolate, her eyes dilated with eagerness. She glared at the provisions as a half-starved dog would do, which completely upset my equanimity.

"My dear lady!" I exclaimed, "I have plenty. By God's good providence I put these things into my bag when I started. Why, I don't know, but there they are; pray eat, and let me assure you that I have ample provisions; eat, and then we'll talk further about what is to be done."

She took the chocolate and scraped some into a tin can, saying, "Ah! it's not myself I care so much about, it's my poor father: with this and with this bread he'll recover, I trust—it will save his life, please God! And oh! I bless and thank Him for this, and you for coming to our aid."

Then she took it behind the other curtain, and I heard her endeavouring to awaken her father, who appeared to be in a kind of swoon, out of which she was unable to arouse him.

After a while she called me in, and there on a rough couch he lay, quite insensible. He was a handsome, grey-bearded man, having an air of refinement I could see, although he was now so terribly thin and emaciated, with face and hands so white and bloodless, that he was a pitiful sight.

His daughter had contrived to raise him on a heap of clothes used as pillows. I saw he breathed, but beyond that he looked to be already dead.

She looked up as I entered, perplexed and alarmed. "I cannot make him understand!" she cried, and with a gasp she fell prone upon his bed herself, and I suppose she fainted.

I was bewildered now; it looked as if they were both in a very serious state, and I neither knew which to attend to first, or what to do for either.

I first endeavoured to bring him to consciousness, then I begged his daughter to try to rouse herself; but for some minutes I called to both in vain, and I thought they were dead.

There I was, completely at a loss,—I could do nothing but stare at them. Was this another horror added to what had occurred to me already? I asked myself. Had I found companions in my solitude only to see them die before my eyes? What could I do?

At length the girl stirred, gave a heart-rending

sigh or two, and turning, saw me. I believe she did not at once understand what I was doing there; but I spoke gently to her, saying, "I think you are as nearly famished as your father; let me persuade you to leave him a while; drink some of this stuff yourself, eat some bread and meat. I hope it is only want of sustenance that affects you. Do as I ask, and I will stay here and try to bring him to his senses, and to take some food."

She appeared willing, but unable to move. I offered her my hand; she took it, and I helped her into the outer room. When I saw that she was trying to take some food I left her.

I had much difficulty in dealing with her father. I tried in many ways; but at last I forced some chocolate into his mouth with a spoon. He swallowed it, and after a little he too revived; intelligence came to him. He opened his eyes, gazed wonderingly at me, and asked faintly, "Who are you? Where do you come from? Where is May?"

She was by his side instantly. "Father! father, dear!" she cried, "we are saved; this good man has found us. He has plenty of food, and he will help us."

At which he, looking alive at last to the state of affairs, muttered, "Food, did you say, May—food? Ah! there's plenty to pay for it; give the man gold, any amount of it, for food—that is worth more than gold to us, my love!"

"Hush—hush!" she whispered to him, "this is a friend; I know he is a friend. Say nothing about gold!"

But he would not be suppressed. He was taking spoonful after spoonful of the chocolate now, and munching a piece of bread, and between the mouthfuls he said to her, "It is delicious, darling. I am better already; it is only food I needed, you see? Get more, dear girl—get plenty of it; pay this man what he asks for it, only get us food."

I spoke up then. "Don't trouble, sir," I said, "I have plenty not so very far from here, plenty of gold too; don't trouble about that, only eat all you can, and get up your strength for your daughter's sake—she needs food as much as you do. What I have fortunately brought with me will sustain you for a few hours whilst I go for more."

"But where do you live? how did you find us?" he asked, looking at me fiercely with dark, brilliant, hungry eyes. "To think what we have suffered, May, and there was food close to us."

Perceiving that it was useless to discuss this with him, and seeing that he was taking food and gradually coming to himself, I thought it as well to leave him.

The girl soon followed, and we drew stools near the fire, where Patch had been all along stretched out luxuriously.

He came up at once and laid his head upon her lap, showing very plainly that he approved of her.

As for me, I was in a position hard to describe. I who had been for many months away from all refined female society, and for some time past had been utterly alone, a dog my sole companion, now sat beside a lovely girl in dire distress, a girl who was without doubt a lady. I was sure of that, and was shy accordingly.

Her dress was serge, it was worn and soiled and shabby, a shawl was round her shoulders, a fox's pelt was round her neck, and she wore heavy, clumsy mocassins, the beadwork and decorations torn and tarnished. Her hands were small and shapely, but they were cut and bruised, wretchedly discoloured and black with bad usage and neglect. Her hair was in spite of all lovely, although it was touselled and dishevelled, looking as if a comb had not been used to it for many a day.

This girl was very fair, her hair was golden, her eyes were beautifully blue, she was tall, and though then borne down with toil and trouble, I could not help remarking that when in health and happiness she would be a rare specimen of a lovely English girl, than whom not one on earth is handsomer.

Now here she was, away back in the Yukon territory, surely the most inhospitable, the most unsuitable, for a refined woman, in the wide, wide world, many miles from all her fellow-creatures, practically alone and starving, with a dying father, and not much hope of rescue. It was an awful situation, hard enough to describe, impossible to realise.

And here was I, a young fellow with precious little experience of civilised life, for I had left England when little more than a lad. I was diffident, too, with ladies, yet here I was, thrown into her company, and, as it seemed, looked at by her as her saviour and her hope!

I saw all I have described, thought all I have said, in a moment, and I considered at the same time what I was and what this fair lady must think of me! I remembered my dress, my dreadfully dirty dress. My face was black with soot and grease; I knew my hands were.

You may suppose that in that country, where for eight months of the twelve every drop of water had to be obtained with difficulty by melting ice or snow, that most ideas of cleanliness have to be given up. Yukon miners, as a rule, do not bother much with soap in the long dark winter.

We two, seated by the fire, were silent for a while. I knew well that I had a serious task before me, and the sooner I started to it the better it would be, and the weather being then settled, I ought to make use of it. Supposing another blizzard should arise, then moving about outside would not be practicable, it would mean death to all of us.

I felt a difficulty in questioning this girl, and yet

I was sure I ought to know more about her, their position then, what they most needed, and in what way I had better move.

She sat silently gazing into the fierce fire. There were several large sticks of firewood ready to pile on, and a couple of huge knotty logs, which it would take a strong man some trouble to get there. I noticed these and asked her about them, saying that she and her father I supposed had not been very long alone, or else her father had been but a short time laid by, as I saw they had a good supply of fuel.

She smiled sadly. "That is the last of it," she said, "and I'm afraid I'm not strong enough to chop more just yet—perhaps that'll last till I feel better."

"You chopped that! You dragged all that inside!" I exclaimed, astonished. "Why, what are you? You don't look as if you could do such work. Is it really true?"

She assured me that it was—that she and her father had been alone there, entirely alone, since the end of the previous September; that he was ill then, and that was the reason that they did not go out with the others of their party when they left. I believe she wished to tell me all about it then, but I knew that time was precious, so contrived to lead her into speaking of her father's illness and his most pressing needs. I told her where I was camped, what I possessed, and made her tell me what I had better bring. I explained that I had arranged to start for Dawson, had all preparations made, so that all I would have to do would be to load my sleigh with provisions and necessaries and come up to them instead of going down stream to the Yukon—that I should be some hours on the journey, and that soon after I returned I trusted to see a very great improvement in her health and her father's.

"Why," said she, almost gaily, "I'm better already. Can't you see I am? and so is poor father. Come and see him before you leave."

I did so. He was sleeping peacefully, and really already looked improved.

When I told her all that I possessed, she was quite overcome with excitement. Would I bring some of it? Should I be robbing myself? Would not I be neglecting my own affairs by devoting time to them? and many such questions she put to me.

I begged her not to trouble about me—that when I returned I would explain all, and she would then understand; but as it was all-important to get what was wanted without delay, I must start at once.

Tears filled her eyes as she thanked me, and called down blessings on me, at which I laughed, asking her if she had met with strangers in distress would she pass them by unhelped? She said "No, she could not." "Well, then," I proceeded, "neither can I, so say no more, dear lady. I'm going to help you and your father out of this dreadful strait."

Before I left I chopped a heap of firewood and brought it in, for which she was very grateful. Then whistling Patch, I prepared to start. "Oh! leave me Patch," she begged; "the dear dog will be such company."

I assured her I would willingly do so if I dared, but that Patch had his work to do; he was a Huskie, trained to draw a sledge; without his help I could not bring much, so it was necessary that he should come with me.

She held out her hand to me, saying with a smile, "It's a very dirty one, but it's the best one I have to offer."

I clasped it gladly, shook it warmly, as I replied, "It's not half as bad and black as mine, but what can we expect in this awful climate, this terrible region!"

"Ah! what indeed," said she.

When I had gone fifty yards from the hut I looked back. She stood framed in the doorway against the light. I called to her "Go inside. Stay there till I return. I'll not be long; keep up your heart and your father's. All will now be well." Then an idea struck me, and I cried, "But tell me, what is your father's name and yours! Mine is Herbert Singleton, of Blumfield, Bedfordshire."

She answered loudly, but in tones I never will

forget, " My father is William Bell of Hawkenhurst in Kent, and I am Mary Bell—but they always call me May!"

Then I shouted cheerily, " Farewell, God bless you!" and calling again to Patch, who was quite reluctant to leave her, I was off.

CHAPTER VIII.

Through the keen air I hurried. It was light enough. The aurora was brilliant. Whether day or night I did not know, or care.

I was enraptured. I seemed to be walking on air. The rough hill-sides, the ice-clad rocks, I passed over with the agility of a fawn. I had companions, my loneliness was ended!

And what company had I found? A girl who had instantly affected me in a manner I had never before experienced.

Naturally, after long absence from female society, a man is easily attracted by almost any member of the fair sex. I quite understood this. But I had never been enthusiastic in my admiration of women. Indeed I had been, whether from diffidence or constitution I cannot say, rather averse to their society, and regarded those of my friends who devoted themselves to them as a bit weak.

I knew this, and yet I felt so elated at meeting this girl so unexpectedly that I forgot all my former notions, and was so joyful, in spite of recent occurrences and our terrible surroundings, that I went on my way gleefully. The awful cold and my loneliness were clean forgotten, the long tramp on snowshoes was as nothing, so, almost before I knew it, I was back at the hut.

Everything that could freeze was frozen, indoors and out. I built a huge fire, I cooked a meal for myself and my dog, and I felt so bright and so exhilarated that I ate as I had not eaten for a long time. I rejoiced in my appetite, my vigour, and health, and thanked Almighty God for His goodness, and not the least for His mercifully causing us—Meade and me—to economise our food as we had, for now I could appreciate the value of it, as, of course, I had not hesitated, nay, I was eager, to share it with the Bells.

To think of that sweet girl in want of food was so distressing, that I would fain have given her all that I possessed and starved myself, rather than that she should suffer.

Sitting by my fire resting, I smoked and dreamed—waking dreams—about my new friends. I thought lightly of Mr Bell's illness. I believed it was merely want of sustenance, as it was with his daughter May. I thought of her as May, which was a lovely name. I considered, I wondered who they were, what was their history, how they came to be up there in that awful predicament, in that dreadful country.

Mr Bell had spoken of gold as if they had plenty; I knew what I had, and this led me to dreaming of what might be. I pictured May in England, myself with such a woman as she appeared to be as my wife. I thought about all that we could enjoy in England, the comforts and luxuries that money would obtain there for us, and I fell asleep dreaming of such things, and slept until Patch roused me. He had become impatient at my long nap.

I had slept some hours. I was pleased, knowing the task I had before me of hauling a heavy load to the Bells', and then returning without sleep or rest. I was not complaining—far, very far from that—I was indeed rejoiced about it. But I was wise enough to remember that I must go sensibly to work—that as their very lives depended on me and what I had, I must run no risk of breaking down or failing.

There was a quantity of food, principally canned meats and vegetables, in the câche which Meade and I built up the trees. I packed the toboggan with a selection, and with a sack of flour, some sugar, coffee, a few bottles of bovril, our only bottle of whisky, and all I could think of suitable for an invalid. I heaped on joints of venison, bear meat, and a few frozen birds I had left. I covered this with the remnant of the tent, lashed all securely, harnessed Patch, and started up the creek.

This was really my first experience of hauling a

L

laden sledge. Patch was out of practice too, so that for a while we did not get on pleasantly.

The toboggan answered well. It sank very little, having a wide base, but the dry snow piled up before it. It was, as they say, "collar work" always.

I had Patch attached by a long trace at first, and I kept closer to the sleigh. He would try to go ahead rapidly. It was surprising the power of that dog, and the more I called to him to go slower the more he hurried. When I had at length forced a halt, I shortened his trace and lengthened mine, so that I was leader. Now he paid more attention to me than his work. If I slowed up or endeavoured to take it easy he jumped on me, barking with delight. No doubt he thought it good fun.

The cold did not appear to affect him in the slightest. He was well fed; but even in the real Arctic the half-starved Huskies pay no heed to it. They sleep contentedly in the snow, with the thermometer marking 100 degrees of frost, as I have learned since I came out that it frequently does on the Yukon.

I next fastened Patch's trace the same length as my own. By this means we got on better, for I could put my hand into his collar and guide him effectually. This answered usually very well, but when our traces became entangled, it was no easy matter to extricate them in the frightful cold.

The actual weight of the load did not trouble us

as long as we kept on the frozen creek, as it was usually level; and after a few hours Patch was not nearly so full of life and impetuosity, and things went easier.

We camped for an hour when we were half way. I made some tea; we had found rather a snug corner amongst some thick pine bushes.

When we reached the hill we had to cross, we had as much as we could do to pull the toboggan up the steep incline. Patch worked well; he gave me the idea that he knew we were nearing our destination, and was delighted.

So, after many heavy tugs, we reached the top, when I called a halt; but my companion was for dashing over it, and slithering down the other side without delay. By hanging on behind I stopped him, and addressed him seriously, angrily, at which he looked into my face, then gazed in the direction of the Bells' shanty, and let out a long-drawn howl.

Here I unlashed the gun and fired a couple of shots, a signal I had agreed upon with May.

She had been listening surely, for the smoke from the discharge had barely crept away ere the door flew open and I saw her wave a burning stick in token that my signal was observed, at which Mr Patch began to bark and howl melodiously: he fairly yelled with excitement, and I had difficulty in restraining him from tearing down the hill.

By care and patience we got safely down, and

drew our load to the shanty. Indeed we drew it inside, for a breeze had sprung up, and it would have been a risk to handle anything in the open air.

It delighted me to see the pleasure with which my new friend examined what I had brought. "What! bovril!" she exclaimed, "and whisky! Oh, they will cure father! and sago, rice; and this lovely tinned fruit! Why, what a stock of things you have; are you storekeeping? I thought you were a miner."

I assured her that I was, and nothing more, but that my partner had been up the season before, had done well, and gained experience, so that when we came in during the summer we had brought a large stock of food—larger than was absolutely necessary—in case of accidents. I added that I was deeply thankful we had done so, as things had turned out. I begged her to use all she could, for her father's good, to say nothing of her own; and to remember that there was plenty more where this came from.

Her father was much better than when I first saw him, but he was still ill and frail. He welcomed me warmly, clasping my big rough hand in his thin white ones, saying as he did so, "Welcome back. I never can thank you enough for all your goodness. You have saved my daughter's life, and I hope, too, I may recover and prove to you my gratitude."

I cut this matter short, begging him to use what I had been so pleased to bring.

His daughter, being present, went over a list of the dainties, as she called them, and was quite cheerful, which gladdened Mr Bell, and they both spoke hopefully of the future.

It was not long before we two had a kettle boiling, food cooked, and were enjoying what she assured me was the best meal she had eaten in that region. Bacon and beans, the staples with miners, had never been satisfactory food to her father and herself.

Naturally it was a delight to me to be thus familiarly associated with her. During my absence she had tidied the shanty, and had also donned a better dress—that is, a cleaner one—less worn and ragged. She had done something to her hair, and had tried to make her hands more presentable. Her beauty was, I suppose, enhanced by this, and to me it seemed that if she was not so thin, and had a little more colour on her cheeks, and could lose the sad look that seldom left her face, she would be perfect.

As for me, I had done nothing to improve my dress or looks. I did get some snow melted at my place, and rubbed and scrubbed my hands; but I could not say they were improved, though a portion of the grease and blackness was gone.

We sat with her father for a while. He was a smoker, but all his tobacco was gone: he tried to join me, but could not manage it, although he was decidedly better. We propped him up, and he talked with me, and then of course they wished to know how I came to be in that part, and how I came across them, and about England; asked if I knew the part they came from, and said a little about where my people lived. He appeared to know our name, having visited in the neighbourhood, so that we got on well. He was very feeble, spoke with difficulty, and his daughter May, as he always called her, helped him out, finished sentences for him, and described to me what she knew he wished to tell me.

As for how I came to be in that neighbourhood, that was easily explained. I told of Meade's discovery the first time he came into the Yukon; how he had returned this last summer, and had brought me with him. I told how fortunate we had been in getting gold, and so forth, and generalised a good deal. I said nothing about Meade's death—I merely stated that he had left me, that I had been alone for months, had become heartily tired of it, and had determined to get to Dawson "somehow" with what I could haul out. I was making preparation for this when I heard the shots, which May afterwards told me she fired every few hours for a week, hoping to attract some one; but of late she had quite despaired. They were certain they should both die. Indeed, as I knew, when the joyful sound of my gunshots, and soon after the barking of the dog, roused hope in her, her father had swooned away, and but for my wonderful advent, and what I had in my bag, she believed he would not have rallied.

I told her my intention had been to remain at Dawson till spring, then return to our claim, finish up there with men to help, and go home in the autumn.

"So I suppose you'll be carrying this out directly?" May asked. I shall henceforth call her May, though really at that time I addressed her as Miss Bell.

"Oh, not now. No; there is no need. I've given up the idea since I've been so fortunate as to find you and your father. You see, I was only going to Dawson for the sake of some sort of company. I have been so terribly solitary; I have nothing to do there now. I shall not be so lonely if you'll allow me to come here sometimes."

"Why, surely," she laughed; "surely, we shall be happy enough to see you, as often as you can come. See what good you have done us; look at my dear father. I wish you could stay here altogether."

I thanked her, and wished I could; but added that as everything I possessed was in our dug-out, which I described, it would hardly be right to leave it entirely unprotected.

They assured me that I need have no anxiety on that score, that robberies were never committed in that country, and that even if any one came across my place it would be left untouched.

I could hardly credit this, but as they understood how Meade and I had come in, and had met so few people, they explained, and declared that I should be surprised at the good behaviour and honour amongst the miners, who, whatever other evils they did, had a strict regard for each other's property. "Why," said Mr Bell, "I've known thousands of pounds' worth of gold to lie unguarded, in view of all passers-by, and it was never interfered with; that was in Alaska, on the American side, where we know the laws are not respected as they are in Canada; and here, under the British flag, we're as safe, oh, much safer, than in England, so far as thieving goes!"

When May and I left him to sleep, we sat by the fire conversing. It was then I told her that I had something like 260 lb. weight of gold, worth, I supposed, £10,000, buried in my dug-out; it would be a serious matter if it were stolen—to others besides myself.

She whispered to me that they had also in this shanty an immense quantity, more than I could imagine possible, adding, "When the others went away they left our share with us, and father and I have got a lot since. He was not so ill then, he could help me. After they went away he and I worked, as I tell you, and our ground is very rich. We picked out as much as I can lift, and there is a dump of pay-dirt, which is full of finer gold, to be washed in the spring. But, oh dear! if father is not better soon I shall despair."

I tried to encourage her. I said I felt sure that it was only want of proper food that had made him ill; now that there was plenty, he would soon be all right.

She shook her head, saying, "Ah! you don't know. It is not all famine; he was very bad whilst yet we had food enough. But I must not despair." She tried to speak cheerfully. "Three days ago we were hopeless, dying really; yet see how wonderfully, how mercifully we have been rescued and provided for. I will hope yet. Please God, father will recover, then all will be well!"

I said that was right. I begged her to look at the bright side of things, and I continued, "You spoke just now of helping your father to mine—do you mean that you have actually worked? Yes? Not underground, surely?"

Smiling, she told me she had not actually worked down a shaft at tunnelling or driving, but that she had done about everything else. They had been working in a mound beside the creek, had traced the gold into it along bed-rock, much as Meade and I had. This mound had gold in it from the surface, under the nigger grass and moss; it was six to ten feet thick, and of course always frozen as hard as marble. They lit fires before it, then removed the dirt thus thawed. It was slow work, consisting principally in cutting firewood and keeping the fires going. She had become quite expert with an axe, she assured me. They allowed these fires to burn half a day, then raked them away, and generally found the ground was thawed a couple of feet in.

Often, she went on to explain to me, they found within a few inches of the rock the gold as thick as plums in a Christmas pudding, and she declared she knew there was an immense fortune in their claim.

I quite believed all this, for it was like our own experience.

When I looked at her I was not surprised at her ability to do labouring work. She was one of those well-built girls that one sometimes sees, more often in Britain than anywhere, who, having from their childhood been used to outdoor life, are physically able and as strong as men.

I could realise that when May was in good health her powers would be fully up to gold-mining or any other work. Withal there did not appear to be the slightest sign of that masculine style which is so horrible to see in women: she was soft spoken, eminently feminine, and one could not doubt she was in all respects a lady.

She knew all about panning off and cradling, and even sluicing, and could do them all. I was of course curious to know how they came to be where I found them, and how long they had been in Canada, and so forth; but I was diffident, and I did not like to ask her. I fancied they had not been very long from home.

I had been several hours there. I did not wish to leave, but thinking I ought to, I went in to bid her father farewell, when they both begged me to stay a while, and I did linger longer, for I really was in no hurry.

We had much conversation, which was delightful to me after my long silence. I found they had no books; so when I told them of my possessions they were envious, and charmed when I promised, next time I came, to bring some with me. I believe it was this prospect which made them willing for me to go, as I pledged myself to return in a very few days.

I left them with a heavy heart, with very great regret.

May asked me again to leave Patch with them; but when I told her that she had her father to talk with, whilst I had only a dog for company, she declared she was ashamed of having made so cruel a request.

My journey home was not a pleasant one. It was very dark, the sky was clouded, there was some wind and drifting snow. It was not so cold, however — it rarely is when the sky is overcast. But for Patch's sagacity, we might easily have gone astray.

So long as I kept my mind fixed on Mary Bell, remembered that I was not now solitary, I did well; but when, tired, cold, and miserable, I arrived at the hut so drear, so gloomy, I felt dreadful, and for a while I could barely look about me undismayed.

However, being fatigued enough and hungry, and the big fire making me drowsy, Patch and I were soon fed and fast asleep, and forgetting our troubles and joys.

The following days I passed far from pleasantly. I sat moping by the fire, only rousing for food or fuel. I did not even think of working.

I could not go in to where I had left my poor friend's body to dig for gold—it was desecration, I thought; so I just sat eating, smoking, sleeping, and grumbling to myself, and longing for the time when I considered it would be right to go to the Bells' again.

Certainly this was very simple of me. I might have been sure they would have been pleased enough to see me; but, as I have said before, I was very diffident with ladies, and, I suppose, much more so since I had lived that isolated life.

However, I could not dismiss May's personality from my mind. I really did not try to—it was a delight to think about her. No matter what I did, or on what train of thought I was, everything led me to that young lady. Her face was always before me, it had such a hold on my imagination. Of course I had heard or read about love, the attraction between the sexes, and so forth, yet I never applied this knowledge to myself. I felt, even after the little I had seen of my sweet young friend, that I could do anything for her, that I would fain secure her continued companionship; yet, somehow, it never occurred to me to say to myself, "Bertie, you're falling in love with her; have a care, my lad."

This is the manner in which I sat mooning by my fire.

I had long since hunted out all our literature and packed it. I went through the remainder of our eatables, finding a few things that my new friends had not received. What more could I do to pass the weary time?

I could not start for four days at any rate, as the weather became terrible—wind, snow, and continual darkness. Not a star or ray of light was visible when I went outside, as I very rarely did, for necessaries only. I can conceive nothing more dismal, nothing more frightful, than this four days' gale. It seemed to me the very forest would be uprooted; the hill shook, inside which I lived. Alone in that awful turmoil was torment. I feared that the whole aspect of the country would be changed, that I should never find my friends again; indeed I fancied it was more than probable that they and their frail habitation must have been swept away.

To live outdoors in such weather, to travel through it, I knew was impossible, and I wondered if any poor folk were journeying, and I pictured their sufferings. I little knew then that there were crowds of people hurrying into this very part—for I was ignorant that the news of these great discoveries of gold had already startled the world, and that all the passes and trails were crowded with folk trying to get in—and most of them what we call "tenderfeet," men, ay, and women too, who had never known privations before, to whom the idea of sleeping out of their comfortable beds had been till recently an event undreamed of. What they must be suffering I could imagine, and what many are suffering now, even during the winter of '98-99, who can tell? although already much improvement has been made.

On the fifth day behold an entirely different state of matters. The wind had dropped; the absolute quietness was painful. I peeped out: the cold was intense, and all nature was deep imbedded in fresh snow. The full moon was shining brilliantly in the south, and the northern heavens were sown thick with stars, and the sky was cloudless.

Believing that some days of quiet weather were assured, I made ready for a start.

Our load this time was quite light, and we went off gleefully. Patch quite knew where we were going, and made no scruple about his happiness.

Decidedly I was glad to be off, but I had some very grave anxieties. I was impatient to know if my friends had weathered the gale. Having cut a large supply of fuel and carried it in before I left the last time, I knew that May had no need to go outside, and so I thought if the shanty had held together I might find all well.

We soon skimmed up the creek—my dog and I—and camped again in the pine thicket for refreshment. Here I shot two black foxes. They had, I suppose, scented the meat we had with us, for happening to look behind me just before we stopped, I saw them in our track. At first I thought of slipping Patch after them; then I wondered if I left them unnoticed whether they would draw nearer, and come within gunshot; but I soon perceived that they were afraid, although they kept after us, so I gave up hope of getting them.

When we camped we left the laden sleigh out in the open, thirty yards away—I had forgotten the foxes. Patch was in the shelter with me eating; suddenly he stood up alert. Fortunately I took him by the collar instantly, and looking under the branches saw one of the black beauties on the load, tearing at the cover to get at the meat, whilst the other was rooting in the snow close by.

Commanding Patch by gesture to lie still, I raised my gun, and from the rifle-barrel drove a ball through the head of one, and as the other dashed away I bowled it over with buckshot, with which the second barrel was charged.

I felt proud of this performance, for I had been talking to May about black fox-skins, and had promised to get her some. It was good to be able to do it so quickly.

They were both very thin, mere skeletons, starving, which was why they had acted as they did; but their fur was very beautiful, and I tied them on the load with great content.

Arrived in due time at the hill-top, I fired the gun again, then very shortly after we drew up at the door, entering with the sleigh as before.

May met me with a radiant face—shaking my hands most heartily, hardly giving me time to remove my mitts before she had me by the hand; and long before I had unlashed my snow-shoes she was praying me to come forward and see her father, who, she announced, was improving rapidly.

He really seemed to be. She had rigged up a couch beside the fire, on which he sat wrapped in a blanket, but looking, as I thought on first seeing him, quite bright and cheerful.

The books and papers pleased them mightily; it delighted me to see them so interested.

May looked ever so much better; she had a little colour in her face now, and in spite of the very terrible storm, which had raged around their unsheltered hut with still more force than it had around me, so far as I could judge, and alarmed them greatly, they had certainly both improved. We talked incessantly.

I found Mr Bell an interesting man, full of information on many subjects; his daughter was just like him in that respect. He was about sixty, and must have been, when in health, an able, stalwart man.

They begged me to smoke, and I having no objection, started my pipe, which caused Mr Bell to try again, and this time he succeeded fairly for a little.

I could, however, see pretty well that he was still very frail, requiring great care, and I felt half afraid that the excitement of my visit would harm him.

But what was I to do? The shanty was but one room: I must either go altogether, or stay; there was nothing else for it. I put this to Miss Bell, who said decidedly that I must stay, that she knew my presence would do her father good, and he backed her up with much vigour, for him. The tears came to his eyes when he besought me to stay as long as I possibly could.

What could I do, then, but accede to his wishes? for indeed I did not wish to go away—far, very far from it.

This shanty was perhaps twenty feet by twelve; the floor was clay. The only furniture besides the two beds behind the blanket curtains was a very rough table of split wood, fastened on to four unbarked stakes driven into the ground. The seats were a couple of three-legged stools, a block or two of wood, and an empty keg. Of table furniture there was nothing but some granite-ware cups and plates, some iron spoons, and a few knives and steel-

M

pronged forks. Their cooking gear was a frying-pan, a tin billy, black and battered, and an iron camp oven.

I perceived they had no bread, only "flap-jacks," a species of griddle cake cooked in the frying-pan. I said something about this, which caused May to say that she could not make bread.

"I'm a first-rate hand at it," said I; "let me make you some."

"It's hardly fair to set a visitor to cooking," she answered, with a smile.

"Nonsense," I went on; "I'm a good all-round cook, really—I've had plenty of experience during the last few years; let me show you what I can do—I'd like to."

Blushing, she agreed, explaining that with a proper stove and the right appliances she had managed when they were in a civilised country, but here, she had to confess, she was a perfect failure.

I set to work, much to their amusement, and as I busied myself they talked to me, and by degrees I got to understand how they came to be in this terrible predicament.

I learned that their party originally consisted of four besides themselves: they had come up the Yukon from St Michael's, had rested a few days at Dawson, and had then continued up the Yukon, and by degrees had crept up a branch river, always prospecting, and without much success until they hit on this spot. Here they had found gold plentiful. They all worked hard until winter was near, and it was time to go out.

The four men were rough fellows, Americans, who had been mining in Alaska on and off for years—they believed them to be perfectly honest.

They had got gold to about the value of £1000 each during the short time they had been working, and were anxious to get out and go home to the States that season, and return the following year.

May and her father were willing enough to depart with them, but when the time arrived to start Mr Bell was attacked by an old complaint, a species of fainting fit, which always laid him by for weeks; so for him to undertake the terrible journey down their river to the Yukon, and then down that river to Fort Cudahy, which they supposed was the only way out, and where they hoped to catch the last steamer going down that year, was impossible.

The men were in a measure sympathetic; they waited a few days, trying to persuade my friends to risk the journey, but May would not agree.

Yet, if they did not go out then, they knew they would have to winter there. Provisions were low; there certainly was not enough to last them all till spring. Many and long were the discussions as to what should be done.

These men being, as I have said, anxious to get out and home, arranged this plan at last. They would go, leaving with Mr Bell and his daughter all the food they had; they would make their way to Dawson, and then hire Indians or others to come up for them, bringing a good boat, laden with ample food. By that time it was hoped Mr Bell would be able to take the journey.

This seemed to all such a sensible and practical plan that it was agreed to, and the four Americans left.

It would take four weeks at least before this help could arrive. It would have to come before the rivers were frozen, or else a very different mode of egress must be devised. Sleighs and dogs are the only means of winter travel there.

The men left early in October; the rescue party might be expected in November.

That month arrived. Mr Bell had recovered; he and May worked at their claim, being very successful, but as the month went by, and no one came, they were very despondent. At the end of that month the river was solid; no hope was left to them of getting out by boat. When December had half gone they felt they were abandoned, and their food was short! They ate sparingly; week after week passed; the snow came and buried them; Mr Bell became feeble—ill; May had everything to do, wood to cut, cooking to attend to, and her father to nurse.

Their provisions were by that time very short, even the frozen salmon was nearly exhausted, and they had no means of obtaining another ounce of anything to eat! and now it was February.

Three days before I reached them they had consumed everything but a little tea, and were actually starving.

As this sad narrative was ended, I placed on the table what I had cooked. "Come, then," I exclaimed, "eat now; let us be thankful I arrived in time. No need for any more anxieties, but to get strong and well, and away from this terrible region."

CHAPTER IX.

Whilst May and I ate, Mr Bell had some oxtail soup, which I had brought.

"How was it that those men did not keep their promise, and send you provisions and help?" I asked him.

"Well," said he, "I believe I can understand. They are not bad fellows, really, but were most anxious to get home to the States. Two were married. No doubt they called at Dawson, and made what they thought a good arrangement; but they could not stop to see it carried out. Very likely the boat was just starting, and it would be their last chance to get off; they could not delay. No, I don't think they neglected us willingly."

"Had you known them long?"

"We fell in with them at St Michael's last June, when we came up the Yukon. We did not come here to dig for gold?"

"Why! what on earth brought you then? Storekeeping? You puzzle me."

"Oh! no. I'm a writer and an artist. I came up for a Tacoma newspaper—to send articles and sketches out."

I had noticed a few drawings fastened to the logs. They had interested me. May had informed me they were her father's work, and this was the explanation.

"But you haven't been able to keep up correspondence with headquarters," I remarked. "Have you sent anything to them? Has anything been published?"

"Ah! that I don't know," he replied. "We sent some from Circle City and a few sketches, but since *that*, nothing. You see we soon discovered there was the chance of making more money here at gold-digging than by newspaper work, and ultimately we got up this Stewart river."

"Stewart river!" I exclaimed, "what makes you call this river so? This is the Klondyke, or a branch of it."

"No! no!" declared Mr Bell, "I assure you it is a tributary of the Stewart, here."

We had no map, no knowledge at all of the geography of the country. We only understood that the Yukon ran through it, having its sources in the Rocky Mountains to the east, and ending in Behring Sea, in the Arctic Ocean, to the north-west. Into this river we believed all other streams ran. I assured him that Meade and I came down it from the east, passing the mouth of the Stewart on the way to Dawson, where we entered the Thronda or Klondyke, which we ascended for fifty miles or so; then we came up a branch perhaps forty miles, and there we camped and had stopped since.

Now, I had come farther up this same stream for ten or twelve miles, and found them. "Certainly," I said, "we must be on a branch of the Klondyke."

Mr Bell was as sure that we were on the Stewart. We could not settle it. I believed that it was, at most, one hundred miles from my dug-out to Dawson, whilst he declared that from the shanty in which we were then talking it was more than two hundred and fifty! It was a puzzle which we could not and did not clear up then.

After this digression the story of their adventures was continued. They told me about the gold they obtained before and after their companions left them, and of the arrangement which was made that they should register the claim in Dawson on their way down, as they expected to find there some proper authority, whether Canadian or American they did not then know. But I had been able to assure my friends that we were in Canada, that all the Klondyke was in Canada; it was known to be seventy miles at least from the international boundary. This had pleased them greatly, for they knew the name of William Ogilvy, the Canadian Government Surveyor, who had been deputed to run the 141st parallel of north longitude to settle this.

Their party being the discoverers of this rich spot, they expected to receive large claims along the creek, and **Mr Bell** declared that he believed they were all **really rich.** "And yet," he went on, "with all this gold, we should have starved to death but **for God's** mercy and you."

Then I recounted what Meade and I had done, adding that I supposed we **also** were wealthy.

After this we talked about our doings in Canada before we came to this far northern part. I told them of my going first **to a** district back of Peterborough, in Ontario, with the idea of settling. **It was** near Buckhorn Lake, very pretty **and** picturesque, **with fine** fishing and game, plenty **of** deer, and so forth, **but** no place for farming; therefore I came farther **west**, through Manitoba—which I did not **exactly** like—on **to** Broadview, **in** Assiniboia.

This caused **them** to exclaim, "Why, that **is** where we went! how strange. Who did **you** know there?"

I mentioned the Birds and Fields, **the** Scotts and Wallises, and I found they **were** acquainted with them all. We spoke of the peculiarities of the **settlers** and the district, how promising all seemed to **be at first.**

By degrees **I** made out that Mr Bell had been at one **time in very** comfortable circumstances in England. If he **had but** been content all might have been well, but his hobby was gardening and farming, and when he married he went into it. He had no experience, and did not possess the gift of money-making, so, naturally, in a very few years he came to grief. May was their only child.

Having some artistic skill and literary abilities, he attempted to make an income by their means. It was all but a failure. They dragged on a precarious existence till May was fifteen years of age, when they had a windfall, a legacy of £3000.

Next to farming in England, Mr Bell's favourite theme was emigration. For years he had declared if they had only done that when they first married they would have been wise and in due time wealthy, and now that this bit of good fortune had come to them, nothing would do but they must carry out his scheme. Friends remonstrated, experienced relatives tried to dissuade him. It was useless.

May had received a good education, and had led an outdoor active life, and her father's plan was that she should go with him to Canada, leaving her mother at home in the little Kentish village where they had lived for years. There she was to remain until they two had made a new home for her in the Great North-West.

Mrs Bell was not so extremely sanguine, yet having still, in spite of all, unbounded belief in her husband's cleverness, she was by degrees led to consider that this would be a wise step, and in the end agreed to it.

From all I could make out then, and have learned since, Mr Bell had not been either an extravagant or unsteady man. He was indeed a great favourite with every one, and regarded, as indeed he was, as an exceedingly clever person. He simply had not the faculty of money-making, as I have already said.

May and her father emigrated then to Canada in 1892—he declaring, as he parted sorrowfully from his loving wife, that in less than a year he would return and take her out to a bright new home in that land of promise, Manitoba.

May and her father went direct to a village on the Canadian Pacific Railway, west of Winnipeg, called Carberry. It was stated by the railway and steamship advertisements to be situated on "The Beautiful Plains," and that land was to be had for a mere song close to the railroad.

On their arrival they found this was an exaggeration: no land could be obtained except at great price, and although undoubtedly it was a "plain" there, yet they failed to consider the dead level, most uninteresting prairie as "beautiful," and only by going "away back" many miles could they obtain a place within their means.

Then they moved on to Broadview, and liked the look of things there. Really, it is not so good a part as that round Carberry, but there are many clumps of wood, called bluffs, and many blue lakelets, sleughs they call them; there is a more picturesque appearance to its surroundings which no doubt caused them to prefer it. At any rate, Mr Bell at once bought a place, an improved farm, with a decent frame-house upon it—decent, then, for those parts—and they were charmed with everything. It was in the fall when they took possession, and the fall is certainly the most delightful time of year in that part of the world.

At once they wrote home, quite elated, to May's mother, telling her that in the early spring she was to join them, for that the long-looked-for prosperity had come to them.

Yet before the snow had been swept from the prairie the following spring all their enthusiasm had vanished! What with the extreme loneliness, the intense cold, and the dreadfully arduous work, labouring work, which they had to do themselves or starve, they concluded that it would never do to have Mrs Bell there. The climate, the labour, the isolation would never suit them or her, that was plain.

In the midst of this sad disillusionment Mr Bell had an offer for the place and the stock. He jumped at the chance, and the next time they went still farther west, to a place called Banff, in the Rocky Mountains.

They reached there early in the season, and with the enthusiasm with which Mr Bell went at every new scheme, when they had been there only three days he wrote to his wife a letter full of the beauty and the glory of their surroundings; declaring that, at last—no mistake about it this time—they had found what they were in search of.

He at once bought a piece of land with a little cottage thereon, and proceeded to start a garden, feeling convinced, he said, that with his knowledge of horticulture he could raise no end of vegetables and fruit, which would sell for an amazing price at the great hotel and amongst the crowd of wealthy visitors who came to that famous health-resort.

There is no saying but this might have turned out well, although from what I know myself of the climate up there I think it very doubtful; but, anyway, this is what occurred.

During that summer they were only preparing their ground; there were very few returns from it, scarcely any profits, but, as they said, when the crops and fruit-trees they had sown and planted had come to bearing the following year, all would wonder at their success.

In the meantime Mr Bell had made some sketches of the grand scenes around Banff,—they were exhibited for sale at the hotel. He also wrote some graphic descriptions of the place; these were published in newspapers in Vancouver, Winnipeg, and even in Toronto.

At the hotel Mr Bell and May met many of the visitors: there were many Americans amongst them, who talked, as usual, very "big" of the chances of making fame and money in their country; amongst them was the proprietor of one of the leading Tacoma papers. He was attracted by Mr Bell's drawings and printed articles, and this resulted in his making him what May and he considered a most excellent offer of employment.

They were to go still farther west, to this same Tacoma, on Puget Sound, on the Pacific coast of the United States.

There they were to live; but he was to go about, up and down the country, making drawings and writing, at what was considered very good pay.

They were now quite sure they would be settled permanently there; Mrs Bell was to come out the following spring, and all looked, and was, bright and promising.

They sold out at Banff, and started afresh under the Star-spangled Banner.

It will be gleaned from the foregoing that Mr Bell was a "rolling stone." The colonies are full of such. They are common enough in America especially.

Only a few months after they were settled in Tacoma news came of the doings in Alaska: I allude to reports of the gold being got there, and the impetus that the trade of the country was likely to receive. There was nothing yet sensational, but it caused Mr Bell to be commissioned to take what they called "The Alaskan trip."

He did this successfully, returning in the autumn, enthusiastic about the scenery and the future of that country. He brought back many drawings, notably one of Sitka, the capital, and others of the famous Lynn Canal.

This so gratified his employers that they arranged he should take a still more extended tour the following season. He was to cross the Gulf of Alaska to Dutch Harbour, on Unalaska Island, some 2000 miles from Tacoma, thence 750 miles north to St Michael's in Behring Sea.

This place lies 80 miles north of the mouth of the Yukon river. Here he was to take a river steamer and proceed up the Yukon some 1600 miles to the Canadian frontier. He was to describe and picture all he saw.

The proprietors of the newspaper, in the open-handed manner of successful Americans, proposed that he should take his daughter with him, on what was considered to be a most delightful pleasure excursion—which is exactly what it was, up to a certain point.

At St Michael's a number of miners joined their steamer with whom they became acquainted.

Their talk was gold, gold—always gold. Our travellers were deeply interested in all they heard about it. By-and-by the idea occurred to them that it would be a grand thing for their paper if they accompanied one of these parties, lived with them, helped them in their work, and thus become able to write, from personal experience, about a Yukon miner's life.

By the time they reached Circle City all was arranged; from there Mr Bell sent back to Tacoma all he had done, and told them his intention in his usual enthusiastic style.

They had joined with four of the least objectionable of their fellow-voyagers.

At Fort Cudahy, which they did not then seem to know was in Canada, they bought a boat and some food, and ascended the Yukon to Dawson, at which, although merely a few shanties and a store or two, they were able to purchase a full outfit of provisions and necessaries, especially " Alaskan strawberries," that is, pork and beans.

They passed by the Klondyke with scorn, being informed by all that it bore no gold—that it was just a famous salmon stream, no more. Indeed, the meaning of its name, Thron duick—Thronda—Throndike—or, as it has since been changed into, and seems likely to be for ever called, Klondyke, is " Plenty of fish."

They travelled up the Yukon, sometimes rowing, at others poling or towing against its swift current. At every likely spot their companions, experienced miners, prospected: they found gold everywhere, but not in paying quantities.

May did not dislike the life, except the mosquito

torture. She had her own tent, and the Americans were kind and attentive to her, as is always their habit with ladies. She had a banjo, she sang nicely, she was an acquisition: they were proud of having so beautiful a damsel with them.

This went on until early in July, when, near where the Stewart river joins the Yukon, they met a party just come down that stream who were all English, knew something of the Bells' people at home, which made the meeting agreeable, and they camped together for a couple of days.

The English party owned they had found gold enough to satisfy them, and showed samples. It was coarse and nuggety. This fired the ambition of the four Yankees, who knew well that, until then, very little such gold had been got: they also knew that this indicated plenty more where that came from. Naturally, they were keen to learn where the Englishmen had found it.

But the Englishmen would not tell: they vaguely declared it was "up the Stewart."

In vain our party endeavoured to get some more definite information; they would only assure them that they believed every tributary of the Stewart was rich.

May had attracted the attention of one of these men, a young fellow of the better sort. For the short time they were together they were very friendly: he talked much of England, and what he was going to do when he returned there.

May told him what she would do if she had made her pile as he had. At which he told her that she easily could make it, if she would follow his instructions, and that if she would engage not to tell others he would give her the route, and ended by making her promise that when she had made all she wanted, and returned to Kent, she would let him know.

She laughingly gave her word. So when they parted next day, he whispered: "Up-stream, about fifty miles, the river forks. Go up the branch that trends north-west, follow that for less than twenty miles, and you'll get gold enough."

All this time Mr Bell had been taking notes and making sketches for his journal; but when these young Englishmen described their good fortune, it excited him and caused him and May to desire to do as they had done, so they arranged to join in with the four Americans, in work and profit, sharing equally. May was, you understand, an acquisition, and could in many ways do as much as a man. So now there were six in company, all gold-diggers.

I did not hear many particulars of their journey up the Stewart, only that they landed and tried for gold frequently, They usually got "a show," principally of flour-gold, but nothing that looked like a pile big enough for six.

When they had gone up fifty miles, as they reckoned, a very likely looking branch went off to the south-east. The practical men of the party wanted to ascend it; but Mr Bell, knowing what May had heard, strenuously opposed this. Having some little knowledge of geology, besides the gift of talking well, he made a plausible theory, and soon got them to agree to try their luck up the north-west stream.

As they proceeded they found gold everywhere, and occasionally a coarse speck which encouraged them.

One day they were camped beside a creek which joined the Stewart, perhaps seventy miles from the Yukon. The miners had gone off prospecting. May and her father scrambled up this creek: it was very picturesque, and he wished to make a drawing.

Whilst he worked with his pencil, May, as usual, poked about the rocks and bars. She carried a tin dish always, with which she had learned dexterously to wash and prospect.

All was quiet, except the murmur of water running over the stones, the buzz of mosquitos, and the twitter of the humming-birds, who were darting amongst the flowers which were plentiful along the margin of the stream.

May having been silent for some minutes, suddenly came to her father, pale, and looking strangely at him.

He was alarmed, thinking perhaps a snake had bitten her. She pointed eagerly, and did not speak.

Going in the direction she indicated, he came to her dish. Then he, too, was excited, for the bottom of it was covered with gold—and coarse gold, too!

For some minutes they could neither of them do much more than stare with amazement.

"Where, where did you get it?" he asked.

She showed him. He emptied the gold into the crown of his hat, and, bareheaded, scooped up another pan of gravel, which he washed, and found to be as full of gold as hers was.

They were calmer now; but they looked at each other with immense satisfaction, for they realised what they had discovered.

"May, my dear, we've got gold at last!" he exclaimed. "Our fortune is made; but, oh! if we could but let your dear mother know—eh?"

They were both in tears, quite overcome with emotion; but they were very thankful.

Every one carried a little gold scales, so they soon weighed what they had obtained. There were over twenty ounces, worth £70 at least.

That there was plenty more ground like it they made sure by trying several places around, and all gave splendid prospects. In an hour or two they had £200 worth!

Then they hurried back to camp, joyful and grateful.

May said she had much difficulty to calm her father, he was so exalted: she greatly feared he would have a fainting fit again.

The others were still absent when they reached camp, but soon returned disheartened: they had found nothing.

May began joking them, and asking if they had found stuff that would go five dollars to the dish.

They dolefully replied, "No; nor any that would go one dollar, which would pay — but five cent stuff was all that they could hit on."

"Two dollars!" she cried. "Oh, that's nothing; that will not satisfy me." She laughed as she cried, "Fifty dollars to the pan is about my figure!"

"Fifty dollars!" one of them replied with a sneer. "I guess you'll not get that round this yere region."

Then her father offered to wager that he could lead them to a spot where they could get stuff as rich as she had said, within an hour. He said this in such a jovial way that they saw there was some deep meaning to it. And when Mr Bell nodded to May, and she produced the tin and upset it into a dish, and they saw the shine of the gold, there was a lively time.

It was late, but light enough; no one could sleep. All hands rushed up to the place, each washed a pan of dirt, and every one showed gold—coarse gold, galore!

No need to describe how they câched their boat, and moved their camp to the hillside near their find. How they built the shanty for May and her father, which we were then in, and hewed a couple of dug-outs for themselves.

Then for two months they worked away with pick and shovel, dish and sluice, almost day and night, till they had secured some eighteen hundred ounces, which gave them about £1000 each!

Then they planned that all should go home together for the winter. They purposed to secure their claim at the headquarters of the Government in that region, which they supposed was Circle City, for they believed then that all that country belonged to the United States. They intended, however, to stop off at Dawson City to ascertain the truth.

It was then that Mr Bell took sick, and the rest of the story transpired which I have already recounted.

Nearly all of what I have so far related was told by May, only here and there her father added a word of correction or explanation.

For the last half-hour he had not spoken. May was sitting turned from him, but I could see his face, and I noticed that he had closed his eyes: I merely supposed that he was sleeping.

When May ended her story we were silent for a

minute. She turned to address him; the moment her eyes fell on him, she exclaimed in alarm, "He has fainted again! He is dead!"

I was bewildered. "No, no! not that!" was all I could say; "he is only sleeping."

Kneeling beside him, she endeavoured to arouse him, but he did not stir.

Again she cried out that he was dead, and looked at me appealingly.

But I had hold of his wrist, I could feel his pulse; it was weak, but I knew he was alive, and told her it was a recurrence of his old complaint—bad enough, but not so bad as she supposed.

I brought whisky, forced some into his mouth, and before long we had the satisfaction of seeing him revive.

May was now blaming herself for having allowed him to be agitated by our conversation, at which I also felt guilty, for had not my visit been the cause of it?

We carried her father to his bed; I sat beside him with his sorrowing daughter for an hour. He slowly came to himself and knew us, but she declared that it would be many days before he would be anything like right again.

It was terribly sad, I felt very deeply for her, yet I could do little to help; and fancying I would be better out of the way, I began to make preparations to depart.

When May saw my intention she was strongly opposed to it, and begged me to remain, prayed me not to leave her there alone, and declared that if I had any kind feeling I would not think of going.

I cannot remember all she said in her excitement; all I know is, that it being against my wish to go, I promised to stay a while, and when her father had rallied more I laid myself down beside the fire and soon fell asleep, for I was very weary.

When I awoke I persuaded May to take some rest, whilst I sat by him, and as she was fagged out and quite exhausted she agreed to do so.

Then when he and I were alone he began to talk to me in a low weak voice. In vain I begged him to lie quietly, to try and sleep, and get well for his daughter's sake. But it was useless, he would not keep silent; he knew she was sleeping, and declared in an eager whisper that this being perhaps the only chance that he would ever have to speak privately to me, he must talk. What could I do but listen?

"You know that I'm a dying man," were the first words he said. I was so overwhelmed with consternation at this, that I did not know what to reply to him.

"Oh, no!" I said at last; "surely, surely not; think how much better you are than you were a while ago. Cheer up, sir; don't allow these sad ideas to take hold of you. You'll soon be well and up again, and ready to start for home."

"Nay, nay, my friend," he murmured; "that will never be. I shall not live many days."

As he thus talked to me I was looking at him searchingly, and I believed that what he said was true. There was that grey drawn look on his countenance which I remembered so well on my lost friend Meade's, and I realised in a flash that I was again to stand by whilst another died.

There were complications here, too, that bewildered me. True, I should not be left alone as I had been before, but what terrible difficulties I should have to face! I should have this afflicted, broken-hearted girl to guard and care for, and what could I do for her?

Of course I am not wishing to convey the idea that I objected to doing all I possibly could for her. I felt so heartbroken on her account that I would willingly have given my heart's blood to help her, but I felt my ignorance and my incompetency.

All this flashed through my consciousness whilst Mr Bell paused to take breath. I endeavoured to make him silent, but he would go on whispering continually. He repeated that as May was sleeping, he must tell me all he could, and he did tell me much, far more than I ever can repeat. He assured me he knew he never should recover, that he was equally sure that I should stand by his daughter after he was gone. He begged me to help her out and home to England, and to do my best to get the gold out too.

I promised, of course. Even if I had not learned to admire May, I should have done that — but here in this savage wilderness, although it was a supremely difficult task I knew, of course I would do my best for her.

To say I loved her then would hardly explain my feelings; I had not thought of it in that light. I only knew that every thought and wish and aim was centred in her, and I was positively desperate when I realised what was in store for her, and what my incapability of efficacious help was.

Certainly I loved her—loved her with my whole heart and soul, but I did not recognise it then. I did not analyse, and here her father was giving her into my care and guidance!

He proceeded slowly, but very clearly, with his observations. "All my life," said he, impressively, "I have been unfortunate. I never made money. I have always been in trouble about that. I'm a failure—that's what I am. My dear wife in England is broken-hearted about us. She has suffered for years the greatest of all earthly trials—the want of sufficient money. She is suffering now, and waiting, hoping against hope, that we will send for her to join us, or come home with plenty. And here, now, at last, we have got money, and are rich; the hope, the aim of my life is granted, and I must go and leave it! Is it not sad? Is it not wonderfully sad?"

I said it was. I tried to talk to him as though I believed he might still hope—but ah! I knew, I knew.

Continuing, he said, "Doesn't it almost seem unjust! We know that 'He doeth all things well.' We know there is One above in whom we have, or ought to have, perfect trust; and yet, my friend, desiring as I do to speak with all reverence of Almighty God, doesn't it appear impossible that He should let me perish just when I have really attained my object, after all the struggles and trials of life?"

I said it certainly did seem to us poor mortals very strange, but we just had to trust Him, and I quoted what I had often heard my father repeat—

> "God moves in a mysterious way,
> His wonders to perform."

Mr Bell sighed deeply as he agreed with me. I tried to cheer him. I urged him to endeavour to get better, to look at the brighter side of affairs, for his daughter's sake, at least. I said, of course, I would stand by and aid her all I possibly could, with my life if need be. I would do all a man could to conduct her safely home to her mother, if he were taken; but I urged him again and again to try to pull himself together, and for all our sakes not to give up hope.

He took all I said kindly; he clasped my hand in his, and promised to do his best, but whispered as we heard May stirring, "It's hopeless, Bertie Singleton —quite hopeless; but I'll try to hide the truth from May as long as possible."

When May rejoined us he rallied wonderfully, and in a few hours had improved so greatly that I said something more about leaving, and again May begged and prayed me to remain with them, in which her father joined with her eagerly.

Most certainly I did not wish to leave them, but I was troubled about the way to stay. I suggested that I should erect a tent, bank it round with snow, use the Yukon sheet-iron stove they had, and sleep in it. With plenty of pine brush, furs, and blankets, I should be all right. For in a tent, in the way I have described, one can keep warm with the thermometer many degrees below zero.

We were planning this when she said, "But why not use one of the places the men made? Come and see."

Wrapping up carefully and taking a firebrand, we two, and Patch, who was true to May, and would hardly allow her to move without his knowing all about it, tramped through the snow to a den excavated in the same fashion as Meade's and mine. It was absolutely dry inside—dismal enough certainly, but to me, used to such a dwelling, it offered a convenient lair.

May returned to her father. I built a huge fire in the proper corner, and soon had a warm burrow for a sleeping-place. It was close to the shanty. If May hammered on her door I should hear it, and be with her in a moment.

For a week Mr Bell continued to improve; May became quite cheerful. I did all I was able to aid them, kept up the fires, thawed snow for water, cooked, and made matters as pleasant as I could. We read and talked, and in many respects we had a happy time.

Plenty of food and firing and sweet companionship satisfied my ideas of rest then, and I was glad to notice that in spite of all the terrible surroundings May was looking well and strong. Mr Bell was able to sit up and talk cheerfully at times; but, notwithstanding, I noted no improvement in his appearance, and I feared greatly his daughter had much to suffer yet.

I did not anticipate immediate danger though, and as I was obliged to visit my dug-out down the creek for another load, I arranged to go, and to be absent for two days only.

Since the night when May had slept whilst I sat by her father, he and I had no private conversation; it was impossible, as she never left the hut. But often he looked at me so sadly, perhaps in the middle of lively talk with her, that I was very much troubled, dreading what was coming.

The day before I had arranged to start he was busy, just as poor Meade was, writing — letters apparently. They seemed to be deeply affecting him. He was paler than usual, and struck me as being still more withered and shrunken. He looked as if there was but a feeble spark of life in him, which a breath would extinguish. How dare I hope that he would ever gain strength enough to take the terrible journey out?

I knew May noticed this change in him: she begged him to rest, she hung round his couch, sadly troubled; and for the life of me I could not say anything to cheer her. She urged him to give up his writing, but all that he would answer was, "Soon, my love—directly."

He wrote only a little more after this, then folded the sheet, and with trembling hands placed it in an envelope and fastened it. Then he looked up at her and me.

His eyes were suffused with tears: I never saw so mournful a look upon a human face. It affected me deeply. What did May feel then? She glanced at me once only. I'll never forget that glance.

Clasping her father in her arms, she drew him frantically to her breast, crying, "Father, dear father, tell me what is troubling you?"

In a loud hoarse voice, speaking more powerfully than I had ever heard him, he said, "I was writing to your mother, May—bidding her farewell!"

"Farewell!—father. What do you mean?" she cried.

"My dear, I have written 'Good-bye' to her. I have finished; and—now—I must say—Good-bye to you—my darling. Yes—I'm going to leave you. It's all right. I have—known this—for a—long time. I'm going—to die here—May. I'll never—see dear England—again—nor your sweet mother. But I know—where my trust is, May. I know that—my Redeemer—liveth. **Tell** her—this, dear —we shall meet—in the beyond. And, May—my dearest—I leave you—in full faith—that you'll— get home. **God** will bless—your journey. Don't fear. I leave you—in **His** hands—and in those— of this good friend—Bertie **Singleton's.** He'll do his best—for you. **Trust** him. Don't grieve—too much—for **me.**"

During this long, sad, and very solemn discourse, May had fixed a stony gaze upon him: her face was white as chalk, her eyes were staring wildly. She uttered no sound until he ceased to speak; then she gave a most piteous, woful cry, and sank insensible across the bed, his hand clasped in hers.

I stepped forward, anxious to render some aid— I knew not what. He looked down upon his daughter, then wistfully at me. "It is well, my friend," he whispered; "my time has come. My sands of life have run out. I must go!"

I put my hand out mechanically. He clasped it very tightly, with a nervous grip, and placed it on May's head, saying most gravely and yet so trustfully, "I leave her in God's hands—and yours. I know you will deal kindly with her, as I know my heavenly Father will. I can trust you. I do. Farewell, dear friend, farewell!"

As the last words fluttered from his lips he lay back, closed his eyes, and after he had heaved a few feeble sighs, at longer and longer intervals, I knew that he, too, was dead! At which I threw myself upon my knees beside his couch, utterly unnerved—despondent—desperate.

CHAPTER X.

How long I thus remained silent and despairing I do not know. I was aroused by May addressing me.

"See," she whispered softly,— "see what has happened," and she pointed.

"I know, I know," was all that I could utter.

It was a profoundly miserable scene in that faraway shanty. The rough walls, the crevices between the logs stuffed with moss and mud; the earthen floor, worn into holes and inequalities; the huge fireplace, with its pile of smouldering logs; the dim light from the flickering slush-lamp; the blanket screen, drawn aside for the sake of air; the rough couch of leaves and rugs, on which her father was lying; and she, standing near, with her hands clasped, her face white as that upon which she gazed, with such a look of woe and despair on it, that it made me feel what no mere words can describe.

Thus we stood, Patch sitting by the fire, turning his head occasionally, with the same look he bore when poor Meade died.

We remained in this position until the pent-up feelings of my distressed companion vented themselves in a moan, so pitiful, so heart-breaking, that I could not control myself. I felt I must do something. I grasped her by the arm, and exclaiming "Come, come away," I drew her to the fire, and made her lie down upon a heap of blankets that happened to be there. Then, taking a stool beside her, I endeavoured to say something to calm her, and to show how deeply I sympathised with and felt for her.

She remained quite silent. She neither shed tears nor spoke, but lay there motionless, with staring eyes, with such an utterly lost look upon her face, that I began to fear she too would die.

This thought so startled me that I suddenly spoke sharply to her. I forget what I said, but it roused her from her lethargy. Startled by my exclamation, she regarded me with piercing earnestness, exclaiming, "What is to be done? What can be done?"

"Dear lady," I answered, speaking with deep feeling, "I cannot tell yet. We must decide on something. Can you live on here alone? I see by your face that you cannot. Can you undertake a journey through this terrible wilderness alone? Of course you cannot; so we must throw all false delicacy aside: you and I are here, miles on miles from any other human beings. I will do all I can for you, we must work together, so try to calm yourself and think what will be best."

She looked hard at me, and, I was thankful to see, trustfully; then she pointed towards the curtain which I had lowered. "What must be done with what is there?" she whispered, and she hid her face in her hands and wept.

I was grateful to see the tears fall, for I knew that to any one in deep grief tears are a great relief.

When she was calmer I talked gently with her. "We cannot bury him, the earth is frozen hard as steel. His poor body will be quite safe here; but could you live here with it?" I asked.

May remained silent for some time, sobbing convulsively. At length she mastered her emotion, and exclaimed, "No! no! let us go away; cannot we start now and make our way to Dawson? I am very strong, I am inured to cold and hardship—let us go; let us start away from this most terrible place; let us make our way to England, and my mother. Oh, my friend, my dear friend, help me to get home!"

Considering how little experience I had had until quite recently with mourning and distress, even amongst men, and that I had never had any with women, I think I acted wisely in encouraging May to discuss and become interested about this idea of getting away. I led her to talk, believing it was the best thing for her.

For an hour or two we discussed the subject in

every aspect, until, indeed, I perceived it was very necessary for both of us to have food and sleep.

I was delighted to see my dear companion eat a little, but when I suggested that she should turn into her usual sleeping-place, she broke down again, declaring that to be impossible. The position was terribly distressing, she could not even lie by the fire and sleep, although I promised to stay by. She showed perfect trust in me, much as a young child would, but begged me not to press her to lie down at all there.

I knew that a good long sleep would greatly help her if she could obtain it, but I could think of nothing to suggest, until she asked me if I would mind sleeping there alone. I said "No," but wondered.

"Then," said she, "I think I should rest and sleep if I could be where you have been—in the dug-out—if Patch could stay with me."

I was surprised, but thankful, therefore we went there together. I made a big fire and left her with Patch, to my great contentment.

I slept for long. When I awoke I thought over the plans we had discussed; I weighed all the pros and cons, and tried to see the worst and best of the position of affairs. I prayed fervently to Almighty God for help, that wisdom and strength might be vouchsafed both of us; I prayed that this dear girl, who had in His providence been put into my care, might be given power and fortitude to bear up against the afflictions she was now experiencing, and the terrible trials and adventures she, I knew, had yet to face.

A great measure of peace, clearness of perception, and courage was bestowed on me; and when May came in by-and-by, I saw that she too had received refreshment and help, and was more like herself than she had been for many days. I lifted up my heart with thankfulness to Him who had so blessed us.

Her first words were brave and encouraging. I could understand that she had weighed and realised, and was not going to give way to useless repinings, but would be my courageous friend, my trusty companion and my help, so long as we were together fighting our way through the innumerable difficulties that we knew beset us.

We cooked breakfast, talked seriously for half an hour, then began to carry out our plans.

Our first duty was most distressing. We carried the body of Mr Bell to the little dug-out I had occupied, and she had slept in. Here we deposited it, covering it with a blanket.

May bore up bravely. I left her alone for a few moments; when she rejoined me outside she was silent. We secured the entrance against bears and foxes with rocks and logs.

I fashioned a cross and fastened it above the door; on it I wrote that it was the burial-place of William

Bell, of Hawkenhurst, Kent, England, who died February 20, 1897, and a few other particulars.

We next secured the shanty. Having removed all we wished to carry away, we nailed a paper to the door stating to whom it belonged, giving the names of the party and their residences, outside; adding that the adjacent claim—describing the position of the boundary stakes—was their property, who were the discoverers of the gold, and that it was duly registered according to law.

As for the gold, we hid it safely: May had no fear of robbery, even if any one should wander that way, which was most unlikely, till spring at any rate.

We packed my sled with the remaining food, apparel, and a few things she required—some blankets and her tent; then as we found we could haul the load easily, Patch and I, we opened May's câche and added to our cargo fifty pounds' weight of gold, which was so much less to remove later, and so much saved in case bad characters should come across the place.

May and her father had kept a diary, so by means of the memoranda I had preserved we were enabled to discover with some certainty not only the day her father died, but when poor Meade "left."

Mr Bell passed away February 20, 1897, and Meade, November 10, 1896.

There was at this season some daylight; the sky was for some hours beautiful with sunrise colours—

and the twilight lasted, though the sun was not up for very long.

We welcomed this promise of better times; indeed it was a great change from the monotony we had so long experienced.

Wrapped to the eyes in furs and blankets, May and I stood for a while impressed with the scene, whilst Patch, to whom cold made no difference, gambolled to his heart's content in the dry and powdery snow.

To us two poor human beings this cold appeared never to vary; it was intense always. We had no thermometer really to test it. We were rarely annoyed by wind; only once or twice whilst I was at the Bells' place was there anything approaching a breeze, and then we did not leave the house.

It was the 21st of February when we started, at noon, Patch and I harnessed to the sled. On the summit of the hill we halted to take a parting look at the scene of so much sad interest to May, and of so much mingled pain and pleasure to me. She shed many tears; but I hurried on, for I knew that her grief, though natural enough, would do no good, and I did my best to interest her in our surroundings, and thus allured her to brighter thoughts.

After this we got on famously. May had a pair of real Indian snow-shoes, and though out of practice, soon got into the peculiar stride again.

We arrived all well at my midway resting-place,

where I shot the foxes: here we halted for tea and food. Out of some pines I shot two brace of grouse.

It had become night long before we reached my cabin, but the heavens were ablaze with northern lights, and we could see well to travel.

Very frequently I blazed trees along our course—that is, I slashed pieces of the bark off with my tomahawk, for I knew when the snow was gone the aspect of the country would be so changed that it would be no easy task, especially for strangers, to find their way without such indications.

We had no adventures, and arrived in due time at my gloomy habitation. A grand fire was soon blazing, and May was installed mistress thereof. I showed her all I possessed, and my way of housekeeping. Then as near as possible to the entrance we put up her tent substantially, lining it with blankets; we banked snow high up around it, brought in the usual layer of pine twigs, lit the stove, and thus made an exceedingly cosy sleeping-place for me, May rendering most efficient aid.

And now commenced a most singular life, in many ways to me a very happy one. Certainly my thoughts reverted often to the past, and I could not help thanking the good Providence which had blessed me with the company of this dear girl to fill the gap caused by the loss of my friend Meade, whose memory was, notwithstanding, very green with me, and whose absence from this changed aspect of our dugout home was to me inexpressibly sad.

May was grieving sorely at the loss she had sustained, I saw. I admired the way, however, in which she bore up. She seldom allowed me to see how she suffered from the discomfort and the misery of the life she led. Instead of complaining, she often expressed herself as most grateful to the Almighty, and to me, for the many comforts and blessings we had.

I was always grieving, though, that I could do so little to relieve her during what I knew must be a most miserable time; yet I had one great satisfaction, which, I admit, completely outweighed all my discomforts,—it was that I was so intimately associated with her, and it gratified me to know that I had been enabled to rescue and befriend her.

For a time I feared that she could be experiencing no atom of pleasure or comfort, but she frequently assured me that she was perfectly content, and, knowing that it would be impossible to mend matters for the present, she looked on the least dismal aspect of the situation and made the best of it, like the good, wise, girl she was, which made her lot easier to bear and my burden of anxiety lighter.

With a woman's tact she made the dismal burrow to appear brighter for her stay in it. There were few articles for her to manage with—brilliantly coloured blankets and a few skins of beasts we had killed was all. I think it was her sweet presence that, to my eyes, brightened matters more than anything, though often when I entered in a morning I saw some fresh evidence of her thoughtfulness and taste.

We passed our days in company, cooking and eating, reading and talking. Oh, how we talked! If some person could have peeped in at us when the slush-lamp was burning brightly, the fire was roaring up the chimney, and on the rough table an appetising meal was spread, they would have wondered. We were far better off, I fancy, than any others were that winter in the Yukon region. Certainly I was reconciled to *my* lot. Still I felt deeply for and pitied May.

Sitting dreamily by the fire one day, talking of our past adventures and planning our future course, we got on to the subject of Meade. I had been narrating how I met him, and how I came to be where I was and what he had done. "Where is he now?" asked May. "Will he come up here again in spring?"

I said "No—he has gone for good and all; he'll never return to me!"

"What! and left all his gold behind? You told me he had taken none away with him."

I was nonplussed, confounded. I did not know what to answer. I hesitated.

"Is there some mystery?" she asked. "By your

MAY AND I IN THE DUG-OUT.

look I feel sure there is some other sorrowful story
—you are trying to hide it from me. Don't you
wish me to know?—Ah! I see there is. Believe
me, if it is something sad, I'll try to sympathise
with you, as you have with me in my great sorrow,
if that be possible."

I thanked her, assured her that it was a very
melancholy story,—then I told her all there was
to tell, even to where I had deposited the body
of my friend; and I explained what his wishes were
about his share of the gold, and that I intended, the
first thing after reaching England, to see his mother
and Fanny Hume, and carry them out.

It was a great satisfaction to me that May now knew
all. There was henceforth nothing hidden from her.

During this close companionship we had talked
on every possible subject,—our past lives, our desires
for our future, our friends and relatives, our hopes
and aims,—until we knew each other perfectly.

Amongst other subjects we had some melancholy
conversation about her father's death, which led to
her speaking about his poor remains. She felt distressed when she thought of them lying in that place
alone, so terribly alone, and frozen. "If they were
buried in the earth it would seem more natural," she
said once. "I believe I should feel much more at
ease if that was done."

I promised her if it could be, it should be,—
certainly before we left that region it must be.

"Why can they not be treated in the same way as you have interred your friend's remains?" she asked.

"There is no such tunnel up on your place—it cannot be done there." I shook my head in doubt. I was thinking, and the matter dropped.

Is it to be wondered that, day by day, as this sweet girl's character unfolded itself to me, I became more and more devoted to her? I cannot tell the moment when I realised that I loved her, when I felt that life held no greater prize for me than the affection of this, my dear companion in those vast solitudes.

That she liked me, I believed; that she felt towards me in the least as I felt towards her, I dared not hope.

Often I gazed longingly at her, yearning for the time when I could honourably ask her the question which was uppermost in my mind—"Could she ever love me?"

In all our intimate conversations the subject of love had never been discussed. I was not brave enough to broach it, and she never did. But often, oh! how very often, we two compared notes about our future plans, how we would live our future lives. We pledged ourselves to lifelong friendship; we vowed that, whatever betided us in the years to come, if, please God, we ever reached home again, we two would ever be in touch with one another, and would aid each other to **carry out** the plans **we** concocted in that gloomy home **we had up** near the Arctic Circle.

We each had plenty of money, or should have, if we succeeded in getting our gold away, and **would** then have the means to carry out the schemes **we** laid. What good we projected to our **fellows!** to **all** poor strugglers at home! What philanthropic associations we would help!

May's ideas of a happy, useful life were exactly the same **as mine,** which impressed me more and more with the desire, the hope, that we **two** might live that **life** together.

That the dear girl approved of me as **a** friend, I could not doubt, but that she **had** learned **to love** me I was not vain enough to believe. How could she love a rough, uncouth fellow **like me, unkempt and** dirty? I was all that **then.** It did not occur to me that she also was very far from presentable in civilised society. Her dress, like mine, was one mass of grease and blackness: **the** life we led amongst the smoke of the miserable slush-lamps, the cooking and grubbing, with no free use of water, and no soap, for neither of us had any left, had caused **us to** become very disreputable-looking beings. **However,** it was **her** sweet face which attracted me. It never occurred to me to think that for the rest she was not a whit better **dressed** or cared for than I was.

Certainly I felt in honour bound to treat this girl with the utmost deference, yet I often dreaded that my strong feeling for her would show itself, and then good-bye to much of our content. For if even, impossible as I then thought it, she felt the same regard for me as I did for her, the difficulty of our position would be greatly increased. Therefore I prayed God to enable me to control myself, and I am thankful to say He did, until the time arrived when it became possible for me to speak out plainly.

For a week or two after the death of Mr Bell I always addressed her as Miss Bell, and she spoke to me as Mr Singleton. It was stiff and formal, but I had not the power to suggest any change. One day, however, we being outside, busy at some necessary work, she called to me to help her lift, or do something for her, and as usual called me Mr Singleton. "Oh!" I replied, "pray call me Bertie—it is time that Mister should be dropped, surely."

She smiled, as she answered, "Surely, surely it is, but you must call me May."

I being quite agreeable to this arrangement, it was May and Bertie between us from that time forward.

CHAPTER XI.

Gold-getting at this time was entirely given up: we scarcely mentioned the subject.

Were we satisfied with what we had obtained? I believe that we were to a great extent, for we knew that our claims were valuable, and we knew we could look to the future proceeds with assurance.

As for May's party's claim, she could do nothing. She believed it was safe, legally registered; and the American partners would return in the spring, and she had all the documents which her father had drawn up to prove her interest in it. With my claim it was much the same; I knew I could prove my title to it.

I believed then that it was only in the tunnel that the golden streak of gravel existed, and I really had not the courage to go in there to work alone, and of course I could not ask May to go in with me. She would have gone if I had, for she had a great objection to being alone, which I suppose was natural. She knew where Meade's body was lying; she knew where we had got gold, and I showed her my store of it in the câche.

Three weeks passed, during which we did a mere nothing: we were waiting till the season was more advanced, when we should have longer days, and so we made ourselves as contented as we could. We had planned, however, that when May had recovered some peace of mind, and had regained her health and strength, I should go back to their shanty with my toboggan, and bring the rest of her gold down.

I did this; I made the journey there and back in one day. She bravely wished to accompany me; it really was unnecessary, and after persuasion she consented to remain with Patch for company. I did not bring all her gold that trip, for I had formed another plan. I loaded some of it on the sled, but I also brought her father's body with me!

I had not told May of my intention, but I knew my scheme would please her. It was a melancholy undertaking, but I managed it all right, and crept silently back, and was able to take my burden into the tunnel without discovery. I left it there, came to May's door, and was welcomed home—it really seemed like home now.

I made some excuse about not bringing all her gold, and later, by manœuvring, I managed to hew out a niche for the body of Mr Bell close to Meade's; indeed I got it all done without her guessing anything. She knew I went out with pick and shovel,

and supposed that it was something to do with mining. Several days after, I told her what I had done. She was very grateful, and went with me to the place, and saw, with tear-dimmed eyes, where I had laid her father.

Shortly after I made another trip to her place and brought away the rest of her treasure; and then, in our burrow on the hillside, there were many thousand pounds' worth of bullion stowed away.

All this time we were seriously talking about how and when we should get away; but as yet there were no signs of spring, further than increasing length of daylight.

During this time a very curious thing happened as we sat one evening by our fire, May and I, talking and planning: she, with a wooden stick we used as a poker, was stirring the earth of the floor about, when she exclaimed, "Why, there's a bit of gold!"

It was so, a piece the size of a bean. I supposed, at first, that I had in some way dropped it there, but when she stirred the earth again and found another piece or two, we realised that it was pay dirt that our floor was composed of! This set us examining, and we soon discovered that not only was the earth beneath us, but the very walls and roof of our abode, full of gold!

We scooped out with pick and shovel a large portion of one side of the dug-out, we carefully picked over the stuff we moved, and it was surprising how many coarse pieces we found. We had several meat tins full of small nuggets before a week went by, and we piled up before our door a heap—a dump—of what we knew was rich stuff, ready to be washed in spring.

However, we two had become so used to finding gold before, that this experience did not excite us as you might suppose. We knew we had a rich claim here anyway, and that May's party had a rich one farther in; we realised we were well off, had each made a very decent pile, and were perfectly well aware that what was of most immediate importance was to get away to arrange for the safety of the gold we had actually got, and legally to secure our claims. Our gold-digging, therefore, was more a pastime than a serious employment—we were eagerly looking forward to start for Dawson.

To wait till our creek opened in June, then float with all we possessed down it on the raft to its junction with the Klondyke, where our boat was câched, seemed at first the only way for us; but could we wait so long? No. We discussed, we projected, we planned, and at last we determined to pack the toboggan with all that we three could drag, and depart at once.

I had all my gear ready—May only needed a sleeping-bag, which we constructed—we cooked a good supply of food, packed all with fifty pounds of gold, and one bright noon-day we started, as we fondly hoped, to civilisation and home.

To those who do not know what moving about in winter in that arctic region means, it may appear strange that we should have made so much ado about this journey of one hundred miles or so. If I had been alone I might have thought less of this undertaking. If I had had a man for a companion, or even if we two had had no experience, we might have gone at it more light-heartedly. But we not only had the terror of the journey to face, and well knew that it was likely to be a terribly arduous one indeed, but we were full of anxiety, when it came to the point, about the valuable stores and gear we must leave behind us, above all our great hoard of gold. As I have explained, the difficulty had been to decide whether to wait till the creek opened and go down with all that we possessed, or to leave the bulk behind, trusting to its safety. We had chosen the latter plan, for we were impatient, at any rate May was, to get away from this awful place—to get home, in fact. So, putting our trust in God's protection, we started.

Our course was plain, the creek formed an avenue through the trees. It was fairly level, though we encountered many ridges and drifts of snow, which was deep; but the weather having been calm for some time, it had settled down and packed a little. Our load was very heavy, and the toboggan sunk in a good deal. Patch and I hauled in front usually, and May pushed, but sometimes, to make a change, she hauled in front; but breaking the track was generally too hard for her. What made our load, probably 300 lb. in weight, still harder to drag was that we could not pull with our snow-shoes on successfully, so gave them up, then sank in, often to our knees, sometimes to our waists; and many a time neither Patch nor I seemed able to get any secure foothold. As for my dear girl, she bravely struggled on and did her best to aid us, but really many times had all that she could do to keep herself from sinking out of sight in the dry powdery snow.

I don't believe we made three miles the first day. Our camp that night was in a clump of stunted pines. We put up our two tents close beside each other, lighting a big fire in front which warmed them both, and really in our sleeping-bags we felt little cold. May's tent being by far the larger, in it I ate with her, then turned into my own shelter for the night.

The following day I believe we made five miles. We were awfully fatigued; and having to put up tents, cut bedding, build the fire, and cook, was no light work after our day's march. That day I saw many tracks of wolves and foxes. I supposed my companion did not notice them, so I said nothing, for I did not wish to add to her discomfort

the alarm of attacks from wild beasts. But I have
learned since that she did see them and inwardly
dreaded what they meant, yet kept her knowledge
from me lest I should suffer more anxiety. She
just "put her trust in God," she said, "and hoped
He would protect us."

For several days and nights we had perfect
weather, cold of course, I suppose it was never
less than 15° or 20° below zero. Then on the
seventh day—having made, we thought, fifty miles
—as we were nearing the mouth of our creek, it
began to blow! We well knew what that meant.
The sky at noon was dark as night, the weird
mountains were enshrouded in mists of driving
snow. Down in the sheltered avenue, where we
were struggling along, it was yet a breeze only, but
even that seemed to cut us to our very marrow
in spite of our furs and wraps: we realised that we
must halt at once, make shelter somehow, somewhere, and lie up whilst this storm should last.

There was a high and rocky bank near the margin
of the creek. I donned my snow-shoes and tramped
across the snow to examine it, and fortunately found
a sort of bay or gap between two huge boulders,
which would protect us from most winds, and a big
fire across the entrance would warm the air somewhat. Here we pitched our tents, and here we lay
for three days and nights whilst the tempest howled
past us.

Providentially there was no snowfall, only banks of it were lifted up and carried past our retreat in clouds, which caused us to dread every moment that a blast would curl it in on us and smother us. However, mercifully we were spared this horror, and on the fourth day the sun came out as the wind dropped, and we were able to move on. But it was awful work: my heart bled for May,—I could not help but show how much I felt for her. I could not refrain from exclamations which, I know now, showed her where my thoughts were, and what I felt. She, dear girl, quite understood: for she assures me that during all this dreadful time her one thought and hope was that in the time to come, if it should please God to bring us out of these horrors, she would be able to devote her life to my happiness and consolation in part payment for what she is pleased to speak of as my devotion to her,— just as if any man would not willingly risk life and limb for any woman in such a case—just as if I, with such a girl as May, was not altogether glad to do anything and everything to help her.

The following day we got to and camped in the cave where our boat was hidden. It was with difficulty I found the place, everything was so deeply bedded in snow,—very different to when I parted those months before with Indian Fan and Jim. We had stowed the boat so safely that it was dry and free from snow, as the cave was. We camped that night in it, May taking up her quarters in the boat.

For some time we had not noticed tracks of any kind; but the following morning, which was bright and calm, I left the cave to May a while, and tramped down to the edge of the larger Klondyke river to make a survey of the route, and to discover, if possible, what the prospects were for our day's work.

There I was struck with astonishment to notice numerous footmarks along the margin. To be sure they were covered with fresh drifted snow, but my woodcraft taught me that they had been made recently. There was a regular path, which looked to have been much travelled. Certainly, I thought, it was a bear-track; and yet, knowing that those creatures hibernate, I was nonplussed. Did the Yukon bears behave as others, I wondered. Perhaps the St Elias grizzlies do not sleep the winter through. Was it wolves? I looked anxiously; the traces were too large, and spaced differently to their tracks. However, there was a well-used way, and I was greatly troubled.

We had by this time become so used to the toil and hardship of this mode of travel, that I was not surprised to find May in excellent spirits when I returned to camp. The brightness of the morning; the sunlight on the snow; the brilliant iridescence of the ice-bespangled branches of the trees, and the broader outlook across the white, wide expanse of the Klondyke; the knowledge of our having attained the first stage of our momentous journey safely; indeed, the very finding of the boat, which was the first link, as one may term it, with civilisation,—did so cheer the dear girl that she greeted me almost joyously as she bustled about with our cooking arrangements. We had promised ourselves a sumptuous repast on reaching the Klondyke, and I had fortunately knocked over a brace of grouse the day before, so we were reckoning on our breakfast.

But I was certainly bothered by the tracks I had seen, and May, noticing my preoccupied aspect, rallied me thereon. This made me put on a brighter look, and in my mind I determined to say nothing, to take all due precautions, and to put my trust for the rest in the good God who had protected us hitherto.

When we started on—gaily on May's part, trustfully on mine—we soon came to this track. Patch instantly noticed it, and would not move on. He whined, whimpered, and nosed it; then looking up and down the path, he whined again.

May was attracted by this proceeding. I endeavoured to pull ahead, saying nothing, merely calling to the dog to come on; but she, perceiving a trail of some kind, hesitated too. "Is it a bear path?" she inquired,

"Bears hibernate, you know," was my reply; "they don't make paths like that in winter."

"It must be caribou, or moose—perhaps there are cattle here, or, maybe, it's the track of people!"

"People here!—not likely." I shook my head as I spoke. "Who would be here, do you think? —Indians? Well, that might be, but I fancy they don't come about here at this season."

"Let us travel along it," said she; "it looks to be an easy way. Whatever made it, appears to have chosen the smoothest route," for we could perceive the trail for some distance winding amongst the scattered timber along the margin of the stream.

Now, my idea was to get as far away from those suspicious footmarks as possible. I wished to take to the middle of the creek, and we did so by-and-by, after I had assured my companion that I considered the level ice out there promised a better road. But she was not very easily persuaded. I believe she had the idea in her head that this path was made by human beings, and she had, naturally, a strong desire for the fellowship of her kind. As for me, I had no belief in anything but bears, and as for getting amongst people again—I wanted to, simply because it was necessary if we were ever to get home; yet I rather disliked the idea, for I knew well it would be the ending of her sweet companionship.

I cannot quite truly describe how I felt just then. Certainly there was an immense amount of suffering in our life, but I thought little of my share in it, for was I not suffering with May? and I did not look forward with entire pleasure to its ending. Only, for her dear sake, only to put an end to her discomfort, her misery, I knew what my duty was, and did it.

We hauled our load out into the wide white lane and travelled down towards Dawson. And as we moved slowly, laboriously onwards, I rarely took my eyes from where I knew that mysterious trail was winding through the timber.

It *was* laborious work, truly. The snow was deep, and it was not packed. There averaged three feet of it, then there seemed to be a heavy crust, and if one broke through that, which we often did, we found a layer of slush—half-melted snow—sometimes but a few inches deep, at others a yard or more, and only under this was the solid ice of the river. I used to go ahead with my pole and sound where I thought it looked suspicious. Often I thus steered clear of difficulty, and often I did not, for many a time the load, and May, and I, sunk in to such a depth that it was actually alarming. She bravely suppressed outcries and expressions of fear. She tried to laugh over these deplorable episodes, and sometimes I saw her gaze longingly on what she thought was a much better road in there amongst the trees, but, dear girl, she never tried to argue with me, or even to discuss the reason for my dislike to it.

Before noon our mocassins and leggings were wet

and miserable. We ourselves **were** in a bath of perspiration. It was difficult to believe that it **was freezing as** hard as ever, and only when, after a few **hundred** yards of easy going, we halted to take breath, were we aware how cold it was, **by our** frozen leg-coverings.

We camped for our mid-day food on a brush-clad point on the south side. It was absolutely still **and** clear. On taking off our snow-glasses the light was so painfully dazzling that we understood what snow-blindness meant, and gladly put them **on** again. I caused **May here** to change her **foot-wear, as** we were staying long enough to dry our **wet** mocassins by the fire. It was a snug corner **we had chosen.** We had a side view both up and down the **Klondyke and** across it.

As we sat, **as** usual **talking of our** future, Patch suddenly stood **up with** bristling mane and gazed across the river. "There's something **over there,**" said I; "that's just as he **did when** we first heard **your** shots up the creek there," and we gazed and listened intently, the dog as deeply interested as **May** and I were.

I, supposing **it was** bear **or** wolf that had thus excited Patch, felt thankful that **we** were on the **side we were,** and got my gun **in order.**

Patch's excitement increased. **He** began to bark. With difficulty I restrained him, and made him lie **down.** I stopped his barking, but I could not make him cease growling. This excited us, and we watched the opposite shore closely.

May was the first to discover the cause. Two men were tramping along the track across the river!—whether whites or Indians they were too far off to see.

The expression of my dear companion's face at this discovery was peculiar. She was flushed with excitement as she said to me, "Come, let us call to them. Oh, how splendid to see other people,—to realise that we are not alone in this dreadful country!"

Laying my mittened hand on her shoulder, I remarked, "Stop—let us think: they may be friends or foes; we must be cautious. Besides, what do we really want? We know our way, and we have all we need. It is satisfactory to know we are in an inhabited land, that is all."

"Oh, how terribly cautious and careful you are, Bertie!" she exclaimed. "I should like to run over to those two men and greet them. But you know best; oh, yes, I'm sure you do, forgive my impetuosity —only it is so fine to know that we are really going home."

The two men did not notice us—they kept steadily on: we could just see one was carrying a pack, the other pulling a little laden sledge behind him. They were heading up the river, and in due course would cross our trail, then, perhaps, would follow it, which was a serious aspect of the case indeed! They would not only find our boat, but could trace us to our dug-out, where all was at their mercy. What could be done? Nothing. We could only put our trust in God that all would be well.

I kept silence to May on these points, and hoped that she would not be troubled by the same fears.

One thing satisfied us both now, and that was that the trail across the river was really made by people, and from what we saw of the way the strangers got along it, it was very much better than where we had been travelling, so with one accord we packed up, and with a will hauled our sled across the river and hit that trail.

The fresh traces of the men were minutely examined. The leader had worn snow-shoes, the other boots—we could see the heel marks. This hardly pointed to Indians, nor old hands—for all but the greenest tender-feet wear mocassins, in the winter there.

This trail was a great improvement; we moved along it quickly—two miles an hour at least!

We had gone perhaps five miles; it was, we thought, getting on for four that afternoon; we were resting, when against a rather dense growth of firs we thought we saw smoke rising.

Now you must understand that we were both in a flutter of excitement all that afternoon. We had said little to each other about it, but I know we felt that we were likely at any moment to meet with some adventure, pleasant or the reverse. We were all eyes and ears. I could see May glance hurriedly and look intently, now in one direction, now in another. Even the dog appeared to be expecting something: as for me, I knew, of course, that very soon a great change would come in our lives, my thoughts were occupied with this subject, and I was trying to think how I should deal with every episode that I could imagine might arise. Once or twice before, we had stopped to gaze around as May or I had cried, "What is that over there?" But up to the present it had turned out to be merely a curious stump, or uproot, or some such bush object. We were on the *qui vive*.

So we considered for a little that we might be mistaken about this appearance also. It might be a wisp of snow lifted by the wind, or some shaken from the trees by a passing breeze: however, I soon saw that it was very blue, that it was rising steadily, that it was no hallucination, and that it was smoke, certainly.

A very momentous time had arrived. "My dear May," I murmured, "that is smoke—that means a camp, most likely of white people. Our lonely life ends the moment we arrive there."

"Oh, what a good thing!" she cried; "but why look so serious?"

"God knows what will happen to us," said I.

"We may find ourselves able at once to go on with comparative ease to Dawson and home. We may find obstacles in our way — bad characters, who knows what? But any way we have up to now, through God's good mercy, been kept from any great harm, and we will trust Him still."

"Why, of course we will," she interjected; "but why are you so sad?"

"I cannot help feeling sad," I answered, "to know that you and I must now cease to be what we have been to each other; but remember that I shall not leave you, nor cease to help you all I can, until I know you are safe at home in England with your mother. Whatever comes to pass during the next few hours, or until that happy time arrives, believe in me and trust me."

"My dear Bertie, my great friend, what is come to you? Do you think I'm going to doubt you, or leave you now?"

"I hope not, indeed, indeed," I interjected.

"Why, amongst these rough fellows," she went on, "as, of course, they will be, I shall want you beside me more and more. I shall, I expect, want your protection and advice more perhaps—though that can hardly be—than I have as yet needed it."

"And you shall have it, May—be sure of that," said I.

"One thing is certain, though, that whoever they are, whatever kind of people they may prove to be," she continued, "I shall, as you say, till we reach home and mother, look to you for companionship and guidance. So don't look any more like that at me; don't be downhearted now, but come, let us hurry on and find out what our fate is."

Then on we went. Within a few minutes we were in sight of a camp. There were two log-shanties and a shelter or two; a huge chimney smoking, and other signs of humanity; a couple of figures were moving about; we had arrived at the haunts of men again!

We had paid little attention to the trail of late, but now noticed that there were sleigh tracks branching from it here and there — dog's tracks, men's tracks: here were stumps lately cut, there the traces of where logs had been hauled out of the bush. Now we were continually exclaiming to each other about these wonders.

Patch was excited—on the alert. When, a little farther on, he heard dogs barking, it was hard to control him. It was their noise, I suppose, that gave notice of our arrival, for we soon descried two or three persons looking towards us, whilst a couple of fine huskies came bounding through the snow, looking anything but friendly. However, they withdrew as we marched on, and were called off as we got close. When we at last halted near the first shanty, one man sung out to us, "Welcome, friends! ye'll be frae Quigly Creek, I'll warrant. How goes it there?"

"WELCOME, FRIENDS."

Oh, the blessed sound! a **friendly human** voice—a Scotsman's voice!

"**Nay**," I answered; "I don't **know where** we're from exactly—up river somewhere: we've **had a** pretty hard time of it. What place is this?"

"This place," the **kindly** voice **made answer**; "indeed, we canna give it a name—it's **just the** banks o' the Klondyke river. But ye'll be prospecting, eh? Have ye had luck? We've had a **wee** bittie. But come—come **in bye**; ye'll be gled o' something hot, nae doot, and the mistress 'll soon get the kettle **on** the boil."

"Mistress! is there a woman here, then? Oh, that **is** grand! This lady here will be so glad of **that**," is about what I said.

"**Ay**, indeed, **is** there a woman! But who'd **have** thocht that one **o' ye was ane**," he laughed; and then shouted, "Hi, Maggie, lass, see here—here's a **lady** till ye;" but addressing us **he went** on, "But she isna fit tae come out into this cold. **Come** ben the hoose; we'll soon mak' a' richt." With that he led us to the shanty, saying as he did so to the other men, "Let loose the dog, and see the others keep frae it. We'll hae to take these freends in, and see to them a while, nae doot."

We were delighted with all this friendliness. We entered **the** shanty; it seemed a palace to us. The **door** was thickly curtained inside; there was a rough wooden floor, an immense fire roaring in the chimney, a table, chairs, and standing expectant amongst them was a youngish, nice-looking woman, beaming with good-nature.

"Did I hear ye cry there was a lady here?" she asked the man. "But which ane is it?" she went on, looking from May to me. "Ye're baith sae rolled and smothered up wi' claes and skins I canna tell."

Indeed it was no wonder the good soul was perplexed, for we were dressed pretty much alike, if dressing could be called the furs and blankets in which we were enveloped.

May's skirt of serge, reaching to her knees, was so torn and ragged, very much as my frieze wrapper was, which I think reached nearer to my ankles than hers did to hers. I wore a cap with ears, and round my neck some fox-skins were muffled. She had a hood, a capote, a part of her outer garment: it was then drawn so closely round her face that nothing but her sweet eyes were visible. We had taken off our snow goggles as we entered.

As our hostess spoke, we drew off our fur gauntlets; this gave her the clue. I suppose she knew at once by the hands which was the woman of us, for she immediately took May by the shoulder, crying, "Ay! come you in here, I'll tend ye; and Tam," to her husband, "you see till him. I'll no be lang awa'."

Then I threw off my wrappings and overalls, drew

up to the fire, and gazed around me. I noted that I was in a good-sized shanty, rough, certainly, but it was light, for it had a large window by the side of the door, and there were pots and pans and crockery about, clean and brilliant, and to my unaccustomed eyes all looked luxuriant.

Our host was busily making up the fire, adjusting the tea-kettle, fetching in buckets of snow which he emptied into a huge iron pot hanging in the chimney, muttering as he did so, "She'll be wantin' water to wash her, my certie—for neither o' them looks to hae seen soap for a wee while."

I heard him and smiled. "You're right," said I; "it is some months since we saw soap, and weeks since we could wash even our hands properly—this is an awfully dirty country."

"Eh! but it is, man," he forcibly replied; "but I wonder at ye, takin' a wife wi' ye prospectin'. Ye're tenderfeet, I daur wager—so are we for that maitter—but I wouldna tak' my wife into such wark, nay, nay. It's bad eneuch for her to stop here in this wee hoose, but to tak' a woman rampagin' through these woods and mountains is no' richt."

He spoke so vehemently, almost angrily, that I could not stop him, but when he halted for breath, "Hold on! Hold on!" I cried; "that is not my wife, nor have I taken her out prospecting. Hers is a sad strange story, so is mine. I found her away back. I'll tell you all about it by-and-by. I can only tell you this now, that Miss Bell—that's her name—Mary Bell—I must take to Dawson and to England as soon as possible. Can you help us?—will you?"

As I spoke my host gazed at me, amazed. "To Dawson! and hame to England! Noo?—the noo?" he cried. "Is the man daft? Gude sakes! d'ye no' ken that it's just impossible to win awa' frae here the noo? It's too late, or too airly, at this time."

"If money can induce you to aid us—we have some with us, and we'll pay you almost anything you like to get us to Dawson at least," said I; but before I was half through the sentence I knew I had made a mistake.

"It's gold, I suppose you mean," the man exclaimed,—rather angrily, I thought. "Gold! well, we've got a wee bit oorsels here, and a tidy claim up this burn. We'll hae a decent pickle washed out before long; sae, ye ken, we're no' in need o' yer gold. If ye'd said grub, now, that would been o' far mair value, but gold or grub it's a' one, ye'll no get awa' frae here, my man, till the water opens in June."

"Grub!" I cried; "we've got a bit in our sled outside there, and up stream there's quite a heap of it yet: if that's all that's needed, you'll find that right."

"Man, I'm glad to hear it, for grub's mair valuable than gold in these parts the **noo**; but I say again, grub or gold, you'll no' get **off** to Dawson for a wee!"

"But why can't we get on?" I demanded. "We've got here; why can't we get farther? My companion is just as good as a man; what I can stand, she can, I believe."

"Man, man, I wonner at ye!" he exclaimed, with lifted hands and eyes. "D'ye no ken that the river is breaking up fast at this present moment?—half a mile below here it's a' under water; in a wee while it'll be just a grindin' mass o' ice and slush, no breathin' thing can live in it, the strongest boat that's built 'd be groon to powther in a meenute—and there's nae trail beside the stream. In the deep o' winter it's a' richt—ye can pull yer sleds along the ice well eneuch; and in summer, when the water's open, ye can get along fine; but just the noo! nay, it's no' possible."

"This is bad hearing," I said; "I don't know what Miss Bell will think. We did so reckon of being able to reach Dawson, to be in time for the first boat going down the Yukon: when will that be? D'ye know, sir?"

"Dawson! Dawson! what for d'ye want to take your lady freend to Dawson? D'ye no understan' that it's no' place for decent folk at a'—let alane a woman. But be easy, man, ye're weel aff here, and ye'll get awa' doon to Dawson lang before the first boat gangs **doon, for** ye ken the ice breaks up in these small streams lang before it does in the big river. I doot if **there'll** be a boat leave Dawson till **the end o' June, and** some say the middle o' the month o' July! Be easy then, **and** bide **a wee;** ye're well aff here, **and** if ye'll let us hae the grub ye spoke o' the noo, ye'll be far better aff, ay, very far **better than in** Dawson waitin'. But let's see what **the mistress and the** young leddy says."

Just **then** the mistress **came in to us for hot** water. As she lifted **a tin of it** from the pot she said to me, "**Maister** Singleton, yer freend in bye has tell't me o' some o' yer doings and what ye **want** to do. Just **bide a wee while;** we'll **tak' time** to settle a'. Ye're a' richt here; **and as for me,** I'm pleased eneuch and thankful **tae to hae sae braw** a lassie's company, I warrant ye."

"Ay, ay," said Tam, her husband; "**that's what** I'm sayin'. Bide **a wee.**"

Patch was **at the** door, howling for admission. Said **my host, "We'll hae him** in, the mistress 'll **no' mind,**" for **I had told him** a little about the dog, and the good fellow bounded to me and was happy.

When **May returned how** changed she was! Soap and water, comb and brush, a few simple feminine touches, a fresh handkerchief round her neck, and behold a figure that fairly dazzled me.

As for me, I gazed at my hands and dress with shame and **horror.** Mr Bain, as I found his name was, saw my discomfiture. "Come awa' ben, then!" he laughingly exclaimed; "we'll tak' some hot watter inby, and see what we can mak' o' you, my freend!"

Part of the shanty was divided off by a screen of blankets, behind it was their sleeping-place, and here I obtained what I needed very sadly—a wash. The sorting of my locks, though, as Bain called it, was a business: they hung down to my shoulders, and a comb had not been through them for many days. Bain lent me a change of clothes, and I returned to the living-room shortly, to be struck still more at my love's sweet looks, my darling's loving presence. Quite a spread of good things was on the table. We had of late lived well, thanks to my stores, but we were hungry now, and our hostess heaped our plates—earthenware plates, how nice they felt—with all the good things she had. There did not seem to be much lack either.

We were joined now by two other men, decent fellows. One was a Scotchman, Bain's brother; the other a Canadian from Peterborough, Ontario.

After this, as we sat around the fire smoking, I told our story. I did not say much about the gold; I admitted that we had got some, but made light of the quantity. May here and there put in a word or two of explanation when I came to her entry on the scene, and was not silent, though I tried to make her so, in praise of me.

It was late, quite late, when I had finished. May was to have a bed by the fire; I was to accompany the two young fellows to their shanty and turn in with them. " And, d'ye mind," said Mr Bain, as we parted, " ye'll no be turnin' oot sae verra early the morn's morning. Yon lassie 'll tak a lang rest, ye ken, sae sleep sae lang's ye're able, Mr Singleton, and sae gude nicht."

Patch accompanied me to my quarters, and thereafter made them his.

CHAPTER XII.

"Hae ye ony gold on yer sledge ootby, Mr Singleton?" asked Bain, next morning; "because, if ye hae," he continued, "I'm thinkin' ye'd better bring it ben the hoose. My brither, here, and the other fellow's a' richt; but ye ken there's a wheen queer characters here aboot, and there's nae tellin'."

"What! are there more people near?" I asked, surprised, for I had not noticed other habitations; but I went on, replying to his question about the gold, and told him that we had some, about fifty pounds' weight of it, but that May had it with her in her pack.

"Ech!" he exclaimed; "I thocht it was a heavy kin' o' bundle when I carried it in till her yestreen. But, man, fifty pounds' wecht! why, that's worth more than twa thoosan' punds. Ye have been on to't rich; we've no got to that here yet. (I wondered what he would say if he knew all.) Ye're askin' are there mony people hereaboot; indeed, then, there's a good number on the creek—there's twenty camps and more—maybe fifty men o' a' kinds workin' on their claims; mostly decent folk eneuch—mony like oorsels, frae the auld country; but there's a wheen suspicious bodies. But come awa' in; the lassie's a' richt, and we'll hae oor parritch."

May was lovely; she and Mrs Bain were evidently the best of friends already, but she was so greatly changed in appearance that I hardly dared to address her familiarly. I don't know that I thought her any prettier; my admiration of her beauty had been so intense whilst she was alone with me in rags and squalor, that it could not be very much increased; but I certainly now regarded her with some awe, and it was with difficulty I called her May.

I, too, no doubt, was presenting an improved appearance. Soap is indeed a great civiliser, and Sandy Bain had shorn off some of my rough thatch that morning, and May looked at me, smiled, and called out, "Why, what have you been doing, Bertie? you are looking different!"

"Not so much changed as you are, May," I replied with a laugh. "You look just splendid."

She blushed as she said, "Well, come, come to breakfast."

We sat long over our food, talking and planning.

We made out that Bain, his wife, and the other two came up to Dawson by way of St Michael's. They had lived a while previously in Ontario, farming. They reached Dawson early in the season;

their idea being for Mr and Mrs Bain to start store-keeping there, whilst the other two were to work at mining, for they had heard that gold was being found in Alaska, and although the rush had not set in, they had somehow learned that large finds were very probable, and they had planned to be amongst the first to profit by the expected excitement. But a few weeks in that queer town satisfied them that they were not suited for that business or life, and when Bain's brother, Sandy, and the Canadian, Frank Fuller, who had been up the river looking into the mining, returned in August, reporting that they had found and secured a claim which they believed would pay, and described the life up there as much quieter and easier than in Dawson, they all determined to go and live together on this claim, and so came up in boats, bringing a good outfit with them, and some furniture.

They built a couple of shanties apart from the other miners, rigged themselves up in some degree of comfort, and here they were, doing pretty well, they believed, but anxious for the waters to open, so that they could wash their heap of pay-dirt and know exactly what it was worth.

These were very good people, May and I were sure, —quite trustworthy, and of the friendliest description; their welcome had been so extremely warm, and we were indeed thankful that our first encounter with our fellows had been so fortunate.

Mrs Bain was evidently delighted to have a companion of her own sex: she told us that, hard as the life was, her greatest trouble had been that she had no woman near her, and she said things which showed us that she was quite sure we had come to stay.

Perceiving this to be the case, I knew I had better explain. "But we must be moving on, my friend and I," I began. "We are indeed grateful for your kind welcome, but we must get on to Dawson, then to England—we must, indeed. I know all that you have said, Bain—I believe that you are correct; still we cannot stay on here. We must get on to Dawson; surely there's a hotel, or boarding-house, or something of the kind there, where we can stay till the river opens."

They held up their hands in amazement. "Why, what kin' o' daft folk are ye? Hoot, toot!" cried Bain; "gae doon to Dawson! gae hame to England! it's just no' possible, as I've already tell't ye, Mr Singleton. It's no' possible for a man to do it; and for a bairn like you," turning to May, who certainly just then did not look much like battling through that wilderness, "it'd be clear shuicide—that's what it would be. Nay, nay; ye'll just bide here wi' us till the waters open."

"But, Mr Bain," quoth May, "I must get home to my mother. I am strong and able; surely, surely we can move on."

"It's impossible; no possible, my lassie," he

answered her. "No; you'll just hae to bide here, as I say, whether ye're willin' or no', until ye can gae doon stream in boats."

"And when will that be?" she asked, and I replied, for I had heard all about it before from Bain, and was pretty sure that he was right. "It will not be till the end of May, perhaps not till June," I told her. "Indeed, I hear that often the Yukon is not open to traffic till the middle of July."

"What a country! what an awful country!" exclaimed May, distressfully. She looked to me for corroboration of what had been stated, or to contradict it, but I could only say I feared that our friends were right. I added, "However, our intention was to go down to Dawson and wait for a boat to leave. From all we hear we are far better off with these good friends than we should be there, and as they assure us we can easily get down long before a boat can possibly navigate the Yukon, I really think we must rest content—nay," I went on, "more than content; thankful for the good quarters we have come to. The only thing is, how can we thus inconvenience these friends? We must come to some arrangement about paying them at least, or else you and I, May, really will start on and *camp* beside the river for the few weeks that we must pass up here. What d'ye think?"

The dear girl looked at me, sadly dismayed; but our host and hostess declared that I was right, and wise in all that I had said—as to "pay," however, that was a business question which we would now discuss. Mrs Bain would not hear of any discomfort or trouble being caused by May—she should stay with her as her guest and friend, she declared; and Bain said he was more than agreeable. "But, my woman," said he to his wife; "it's no' want o' wull, it's just want o' means, ye ken. We can buy naething here—there's just food enough to last you and me and Sandy and Frank till we expect the river will open. How can we promise to feed these freends? It's just that, and only that, which fashes me."

Here I could simplify matters. "See here," said I; "on our sled is food enough for we two for several weeks, and up at our dug-out, that I've told you of, we have quite a food-supply, enough for a dozen people for several months. I will make an effort and go up there and fetch a load of it. Will that do?"

"Do? why, of course it will," they replied; "fine that. In a couple of weeks or so the upper waters will be free from ice, then twa o' ye can gang up quite easy and bring your boat down, laden. So, it's a' settled. You, Miss Bell, will stay in this hoose wi' me and my wifie here; and you, Mr Singleton, will chum up wi' Frank and Sandy; but, of coorse, oor meals will a' be thegither eaten here."

Thus it was arranged; and after the day's discussion—for we took all day coming to this decision—May and I, having a moment's privacy, satisfied each other that it was wisely settled.

Of course I was not idle. I went to work next day with the men. The diggings were about a quarter of a mile from Bain's shanties, on a little creek running into the Klondyke. From a couple of hundred yards above the junction, claims were pegged out for half a mile or more, and tents and rough cabins were set up along its margin. It was not thickly timbered there, and what trees there were they were cutting down for mining purposes and fuel. It was very quiet, as most of the miners were working underground, and had shelters over their shafts and windlasses—so little was visible.

Heaps of gravel were being piled upon each claim, but it would not be till summer, when they were washing, that any real excitement would be seen. Most of these heaps were reported to be very rich.

The Bains' claim was some distance up the creek. They had traced the pay-streak in from a bar on it. They had not sunk a shaft, but were removing the entire alluvium down to bed rock. They had four feet of pay-dirt, and only about the same quantity of moss, muck, and gravel from the surface down to it.

They worked in the usual way through the solidly

frozen ground, with fires. I, being well used to axe-work, went in for cutting the fuel for the purpose.

The claim-owners were paying as much as ten dollars a-day, gladly, to any one who would work for them. There were very few who would do so for wages, though; so, as I did not reckon to take any pay from our friends, I felt that May and I were not under so great obligation to them. Moreover, the stores we had brought, and the supply we possessed up-stream, was of the utmost value.

It was a comfortable life we passed now—at least it seemed so to me after my experience; and May assured me that she was not dissatisfied—except, naturally, at the delay in getting homewards. But as that certainly could not be helped, we were both making ourselves contented.

I met May at every meal, and passed the evenings in her company, but never alone. Mrs Bain never went outside the shanty. But occasionally, rarely, when it was what we called fine, May muffled up and came out, when she and I were able to compare notes, and plan.

One very great perplexity we had, was about our gold câched up the creek. As yet we had only admitted to our friends that we had the fifty pounds' weight of it. We had spoken of our claims, certainly, and had said how sure we were that they would pay; but they had no idea of their richness.

May and I talked whenever we had a chance

together about this matter: she was all for telling these new friends and getting their advice. She was certain that they were perfectly true and trusty. So was I, and yet I advised caution. We could not easily decide.

Mrs Bain was about eight-and-twenty,—a well-read, clever Scotswoman, and very religious. She had in Scotland considerable lung trouble. Ontario had helped her, and now, strange as it may appear, in the intense cold and dreariness of this Yukon country she had lost all signs of weakness, and considered herself a strong woman. Still, her husband objected to her putting her head outside the place. "My woman," he was often saying, "you see to a' things ben the hoose; we'll see that ye get all ye want—wood, and snow for watter and a' things; and noo that ye hae this bonnie lassie for company, ye'll do fine."

The weather was quite calm for two weeks after we arrived—cold, of course, except at midday for an hour or so. But we could see signs of spring coming. The snow was packing; there were bare patches on the hills and on the creek; the slush beneath the upper layer of snow was deeper and softer. I had the curiosity to go out on to the Klondyke, and I found it very much worse than when May and I were on it. In places the ice was burst up, and I realised that it would have been impossible for us to move along it if we had

R

been unwise enough to start. We would surely have had to camp somewhere on the way, and live in misery, perhaps many miles from any help. We were very far better off than that.

A couple of miles up the Klondyke the ice was at this time broken up, and by the strong current was being piled up on the bars and banks. Every day made a change, and we saw that we could soon bring our boat down as was planned. Therefore the time had arrived when we must make our journey up to my place, and so it became absolutely necessary that we two should settle what should be done about the gold.

I fortunately got May outside, and had a talk with her about it. "Shall I leave it where it is?" I asked, "and trust all will be well; or shall I try to bring some down secretly?"

She was all for telling the truth to the Bains and Frank, and bespeaking their help. I was as certain as she was of their honesty and integrity, but I knew what a fascination gold has, and I thought it just possible that the knowledge of our riches might affect them, and cause them to do something unpleasant, and complicate affairs in some way. But May would not hear of this. "No, no!" she exclaimed; "they are good, true people. I say tell them all, and get their help."

We talked this over for some time, and the result was that when we were gathered round the fire that evening, I made a clean breast of it. I told them what Meade and I had found, and what May and her father had, and that, besides the stock of food which I had told about, there was this immense quantity of gold, and that the fifty pounds we had with us then was merely a sample of it.

Our story staggered them, especially our coming away and leaving it unprotected. We had, May and I, to go over again and again the history of our find, and the statement of the actual quantity we had obtained. We were obliged to explain about the lay of the gravel in which we had found it, and to give all the information we could about the likelihood of there being more about both places.

As to this latter point we assured them that we believed the whole district was very rich. We told them what we had discovered even inside my dug-out, and before we separated that night they all became so excited that I foolishly began to dread they would do something troublesome.

Such is the effect of gold. I suppose nothing else could have made me suspicious of such worthy people.

The following morning there was more discussion and more enthusiasm. In the end it was settled that Sandy, Frank, and I should go up, taking two sleds, with Patch and their two dogs, who were trained, to help in hauling them. As they knew the Canadian mining laws quite thoroughly, which we did not, they would help me to mark out our claim properly, then they would stake out one for themselves—for, as Bain said, "The moment it is known in Dawson what you have found up there, there'll be such a crowd o' folk rush up that it'll be better to hae freends alongside ye than strangers."

This being quite true, we were well pleased.

We also arranged to go on up to May's claim, and **mark** that **out** properly too. We laid some other plans, which will be explained later **on**.

The trail up **the** Klondyke,—which May and I had not used when we came **down**, because I fancied it was a bear-path,—it appeared, was the way by which all the miners went up the river in winter. **It led** up to the head, where for years a little mining had been going on. During the time we had **been** at Bain's several parties had come down **it**. Their reports had not been very favourable. I had questioned some of them closely, being anxious to discover if any of them **had** gone **up what** I called **Meade's Creek; but so far as I could** make out, **no** one had. They described some tracks they saw going up at one place though, which seemed to me **to be ours,** and they rather jeered at the idea of any one having been foolish enough to go there prospecting, as they declared, as all did then, that no gold, to pay grub even, was to be had, except clear up at the head of the main Thronda stream. How little they knew; and **how** differently they talk about it **now**!

We were off at once. The trail we found fairly good up to where our boat was cached. Hereabouts the ice was disappearing from the stream. We saw we could easily get her out and afloat, which was satisfactory. We camped there that night.

Turning up **Meade's** Creek **in the morning**, it was all but free of ice; we found the way **very** bad beside it. The **snow was gone** in some places, but having light loads, we pushed on slowly but surely.

We were, however, very much disgusted to notice the tracks of others having gone up rather recently. Had **they followed** May's and mine, we wondered? **Had they come to** our **claim, and found our stores and gold?** I **was** quite anxious, as **you** may guess.

Two **persons had gone up:** one wore moccasins, and drew **a sled**; the other wore boots—we saw the heel marks.

This brought to my mind **instantly the two May** and I had seen when we were coming down. **I was** sure they were the same men's tracks.

Sandy knew them, too. **He** said they were all right, and decent fellows—the moccasins were worn by an old miner he called White-eyed Williams, and the **boots by an** Englishman who **had** come up during winter, who foolishly, he thought, **stuck** to knee-high boots. His name, he said, was Coney.

Coney! why, that was the name, I remembered, of

the young fellow who had showed us some attention, Meade and me, when we arrived at Skagway. I wondered if it could be the same.

We hurried on excitedly, full of anxiety, for if they had discovered we had found gold there rich, there was no telling what they might be doing.

With our light loads we got on very much faster than May and I did, in spite of the horrid state of the trail—half slushy snow, half morass; frozen every night, thawing every day.

On the fourth evening out, when we were camped a few miles only below our old den, as darkness fell we perceived a fire burning in the distance. On investigation we found it to be two men halted on their way down. Sandy hailed them. It was White-eyed Williams and Coney.

I at once recognised the latter; he did not remember me, or our former meeting.

We sat by their huge fire beside their one little tent, smoking and comparing notes. They informed us that they had tried here and there for many miles up the main river, as they called the Klondyke, and had had no luck. They had seen a trail (my trail and May's) coming down this creek as they passed the mouth of it on their outward journey. They supposed it was just a couple like themselves who had been prospecting, and were returning disgusted. But on their own way back, unsuccessful, when they noticed the traces again, they followed them up, just for curiosity, to ascertain what their makers had been doing up there.

This was intensely interesting to me, you may be sure.

Said Coney, "Not far up from here—we left this afternoon—we came to a dug-out; near it was the mouth of a big drive, a regular tunnel. A lot of work had been done there. The owners had only lately left—we made that out; and there was a notice stuck on the door of the shack, who it belonged to. We did not force our way into the crib, nor did we try their pile of pay-dirt, nor enter their tunnel, of course; but you bet we tried some stuff from the bankside along the creek, and, my word for it, friends, these fellows have hit on it good! White-eye and I washed out a few pans only—see, here's some of it," and he showed a handful of shining bits. "Then we marked out a claim, and are hurrying down to register it, and if you men are wise you'll do the same to-morrow, for, depend upon it, it is very rich along the creek up there."

I could hardly keep silent, I was in such an excited state on hearing this story. Sandy was staring at me, and Frank asked, "What were the names of the owners of this claim, then, which were stuck on the door?"

"It was Herbert Singleton and Percy Meade," said Coney.

"Well, I'm Herbert Singleton," I exclaimed; "it's

my claim where you have been. We're on our way there now to bring away some grub, and to see that all is right."

"Well met!" Coney cried. "Well met! Now we shall hear all about it. We know it's all right up there, but tell us all about it. Honour bright, we'll keep it all as dark as possible."

So what could I do but admit that I had a good claim there. I was as reticent as I could be, though. I thanked them for not having disturbed anything, and begged them for their own sake and ours to say as little about the place as might be, either on the creek where the Bains were, or at Dawson, when they reached it. This they promised willingly enough.

We stopped with these fellows quite a time, talking things over, and arranging plans. We sent a message back to the Bains by them. I pencilled a few lines to May, and we left them full of jubilation.

When we were alone we did nothing but congratulate one another upon the good fortune of our secret being discovered by two men whom my companions were quite sure were honest fellows, though up to that time they had been unlucky in finding gold.

Coney, I perceived, was a well-bred Englishman; in conversation he had mentioned names and places at home which assured me he was that. But that country, like every out-of-the-way corner of the globe, holds many such, many reliable enough and honourable, but also many just "ne'er-do-weels," and failures of **all sorts,** who have become blacklegs and gamblers. It **is** never wise to trust any man, **certainly not** a fellow-countryman, until you know.

However, this one had said a few things which **made me** think **well of** him, so I did not regret that above our claim, where they had marked theirs out, we might hope to have decent neighbours; whilst below it, where, **no** doubt, **Frank and** Sandy Bain would stake out theirs, we should have friends.

We three were off by daybreak the following morning, soon reached our destination, and found all right and untouched by man **or** beast. The balance **of** the day we were occupied in examining the surroundings, pegging **the claim out properly,** testing the gravel about, and deciding just where my friends should take **their** claim. **We** passed the night **in** the dreary den where Meade **and I** had spent those terrible days, and where May **and** I had sojourned so long.

Little had I dreamed of ever returning to it again. Surely I had not imagined it possible to be there again so soon.

Having told my friends about Meade's death, **and** May's father's, and where **I** had deposited their bodies, we proceeded, first thing next morning, to carry out **our** plan. It was to dig a grave on a knoll near by and bury them decently therein.

To **dig** this grave it was necessary to proceed

exactly as we did in mining. We lit a huge fire, when we had chosen the place, and left Frank to attend to it, whilst Sandy and I went up to May's claim, as we had all got to call it.

We arrived there late that evening. We only took our sleeping-bags and a bit of food with us; Patch hauled them on a sled. The good old dog knew the road well. I have not mentioned him lately—he was still May's pet and mine, as he was every one's.

Early next morning we marked out this claim, properly too, the size we knew six people were entitled to. We rectified the notices on the shanty door also, and, making no delay, hurried back to Frank.

We found that he had managed to get a grave sunk deep enough during our absence, and the following morning we reverently disinterred the bodies of my friends, took them up the hill, and laid them side by side in it. By May's desire I read the proper service from her own prayer-book, with which she had entrusted me for the purpose.

We covered them in, raised a cairn of heavy rocks and boulders over them, and on the summit erected, very securely, a big wooden cross that we had fashioned for the purpose down at Bain's, and had brought up with us. On it we had carved the names and so forth of those who were interred there.

There, surely, it will remain and be respected for many a day. Although, no doubt, all the ground about there will be turned up by miners, they will not disturb the spot made sacred by that grave.

That night we opened our câche, and took our gold from its hiding-place. My companions only then appeared able to comprehend that all was true that May and I had told them. How they gloated over it! How they marvelled at it! As for me, I was more and more thankful at our good fortune. For now I felt confident that if God spared our lives, we should get all safely out, and I had it impressed upon me more and more that May would learn to love me, and I was looking forward with hope, with confidence, to the time when she and I, in England, would enjoy it all together.

I have said little about the state of my mind on this subject. All I need say now is, that the more I saw of her, the more I loved her. My thoughts were ceaselessly of her, waking or sleeping. I longed eagerly for the time when I could tell her of my heart's desire, and beg from her one word of hope.

There had been no opportunity of late for private conferences, for love-making. Many a time I yearned to tell her all, for now that she had others about her, I felt I could with honour speak to her. It was quite different when we were living and journeying alone: then I felt constrained to be silent. Yet now that I felt free to tell all, there was no opportunity.

In that bitter climate, when we happened to be out together, it was as much as we could manage to discuss pure business affairs; to talk to her of love would have been impossible, and sadly out of place. Yet in spite of all these difficulties, now and again, I know, a word or look escaped me, against my will perhaps, which showed the dear girl what I was thinking of; whilst the words of warmest friendship and looks of love she gave me frequently, led me to believe that when the right time came I should win her. I was impatient, but very happy at the bright prospect before me.

With our two sleds heavily laden with gold and stores we hurried down. Well, we could not hurry much, for the trail was terrible; the snow was nearly all gone. In places it was all that we three and the dogs could do to move one sled. Once we had to unpack and portage. It took us three days' hard work to get down to our boat, but then we gladly saw that we could do the rest of the journey in her. And so we did, getting down stream in capital time, bringing her and her lading safely to the beach in front of Bain's shanty early one morning before they were out of bed.

I need not say we had a glorious welcome. I need not stay to tell all we did and said. My darling was the first to grasp my hand and joyfully greet me. Fain would I have clasped her to my heart and told her then and there how much I loved her, and how I yearned for the time to come when we should be in deed and in truth all the world to one another.

It was an exciting time. We spent all that day stowing away the gold safely, explaining about our journey, about the claims Sandy and Frank had marked. White-eyed Williams and Coney came in to supper; we turned out some of our eatables and had a glorious time.

And before we separated, Bain said he thought it would be very nice and proper if we were to render thanks to where we all knew thanks were due for all the mercies and good fortune that had been vouchsafed to us. So, having read an appropriate chapter or two from the good old Book, he prayed a prayer of praise and gratitude, and we all felt the better for this simple service.

CHAPTER XIII.

Now, quickly, the weather changed and the spring advanced. We had some days almost mild, sometimes it rained instead of snowed, often a warm wind blew. At any rate it felt warm to us. Anywhere else, I suppose, we should have called it winter, but, after our experience, we thought this prime, for we knew that spring was at hand.

The creek, the Klondyke even, were becoming quite free of ice, water lay about in pools: certainly every night all was frozen again, but whenever the sun burst through the mists and murk they thawed, and it was a teaser to get about. To travel down them, either by water or by trail, was simply impossible.

White-eye and Coney, who had been very boastful of the way in which they intended to go "right off" to Dawson to register their claim, had to give it up.

We had many interesting discussions during this time about the future means of travel in that region. Supposing these gold discoveries were as great and as extensive as we had reason to expect they would be, we wondered what would be arranged for easier entrance and exit. Should large crowds of people rush in, which we quite expected, how were they to be fed? How were stores to be brought?

Bain, a long-headed Scotsman, pronounced dead against the St Michael's route. The idea of journeying 1800 miles up the Yukon, after the long and dangerous voyage of 2750 miles by ocean steamers across the Gulf of Alaska into Behring Sea, was absurd, he thought, especially as he averred that the river is only open for about three months, from July to October, and was then so full of bars, sandbanks, and shallows, snags and currents, that it is a most hazardous stream to navigate.

When they came up, they were several times nearly being wrecked, and they passed half-a-dozen boats and scows fast on sandbanks, where they most probably still remained.

I had fully described the way Meade and I, with our two Indians, had reached the Klondyke. A road over the White Pass I knew could be made with comparative ease, and from what we had heard of the Chilcoot Pass, that, too, might be made available for traffic.

Skagway, the landing-place for the White Pass, was on tidal water, open always; it was easy to land people and goods there. Then the distance across the pass being only about forty-three miles to the head waters of the Yukon, say Lake Bennet, it did appear that must be the best road in. As for the Miles Cañon and the White Horse Rapids — the only serious obstacles on the way thence to Dawson — we considered that with very little engineering skill, and but small outlay, they would be overcome, either by tramways or short canals. Seeing that the distance from Victoria, on Vancouver Island, to Dawson *viâ* St Michael's is altogether about 4500 miles, and *viâ* Skagway and the White Pass is but 1600, this did seem common-sense.

We had amongst our acquaintances on this diggings one or two Canadians who had been about this region for years. They were always talking about a route "all Canadian." All these landing-places I have mentioned are in American territory. We dispute that certainly. However, the Yankees are in possession, and it is quite possible that they will continue to be so.

But it seemed to Bain — and I certainly agreed with him — that the Canadian route they talked of had very little advantage, if any, over the White or even the Chilcoot Pass. Their idea was to make Telegraph Creek, which is in Canada, 150 miles up the Stickeen river from Fort Wrangel, the port for this country. They said that it had been already long used for traffic with the Cassiar gold mines, and asserted that there is a trail from it to Teslin Lake, down which there is good navigation to the Hootalinqua river, and so to the Yukon and Dawson. The distance from Victoria they supposed to be about 1500 miles.

But here, it seemed to us, were exactly the same difficulties, if not greater ones, than on the other routes.

Bain, who appeared to have studied the geography of this region before they entered it, having had the opportunity of examining the best maps available in Victoria, was strong in the opinion that the Canadian Government should, and would ultimately, build, or cause to be built, a railway from a really undoubted Canadian port, all through Canadian territory, to Dawson.

If this goldfield proved to be what we expected, it would have to be done some day. His idea was that there should be a railway from Fort Simpson, in Canada, where there is open water all the year round for ocean ships, to Teslin Lake, about 400 miles in. Indeed, he went so far as to maintain that this railway should be continued right down to Dawson, for only by this means could the country be properly developed.

No roads for teams could ever be satisfactory. The forage for cattle having all to be imported would alone cause this to be so. On the long journey animals could do little more than haul their own food.

Certainly, if easy roads were made across the

s

passes, if steamers were put upon the lakes, if ways were made for getting past the cañons and rapids, large quantities of stores could be taken in during three or four months of open water. But he stuck to it, that only a railway will do all that must be done, if this Canadian Yukon country is to be exploited as it deserved to be. Quartz reefs rich in gold were already known to exist. Copper had been found too—there appeared to be immense deposits of it. Coal existed also, and it is recognised that the supply of wood fuel for mining and domestic purposes will soon run short—a most important consideration, perhaps the most important of all. These reefs and copper and coal mines cannot be worked without heavy machinery, which cannot be handled or conveyed in by waggon or sleigh, neither can the products of these mines. A railway, and only a railway, could solve the problem.

Whether one will "pay" or not is quite another matter.

In California, Australia, and those parts of Canada in which gold has hitherto been found abundantly, causing a large influx of people, the result has been that many who have made much or little have remained there, settling on the land or going into business, and so permanently developing the country.

In the Yukon this can never be. Gold especially, and copper, and probably some other metals, are alone the product of the country. Land being absolutely unproductive, and the climate terrible, no one will make a permanent home there.

With such discussions, and much beside of purely local interest—such as how Bill the Butcher's claim was looking, and if Tom the Tinker had found any coarse gold in the hole he had last sunk, or what the chances were of Mississippi Sam and his partner the Baltimore Oriole finding good gold up at the creek-head where they had gone prospecting, when they may be expected back, and so forth,—with such topics of interest, I say, as these the time passed quickly.

The increased heat of the sun was perceptibly lessening the snow on the ranges, the creeks were rising, the ice had disappeared, or was piled on the banks, where it was thawing rapidly. There was a great change perceptible—a change which was a source of constant interest to all of us; and to May and me it was a very great relief to see the road gradually opening for us to get away.

During this time we had become pretty intimate with "Coney." I learnt his proper name, found him a very genial companion—one very like my poor lost Meade—and I liked him; so did we all.

He had been unfortunate, and had not found a payable claim until now; and even now, the one he and White-eyed Williams had marked above us, though it promised well, had yet to be proved. However, his hopes were high, and I could not help giving him every encouragement. Knowing I was going home to England, he was most anxious that I should take letters from him to his people— nay, that I should visit them; and I, arguing that if not all right, he would hardly have done this, concluded that he was a reliable man. Bain thought as I did, and it resulted that I, with May's entire accord, put all the affairs connected with our claims into their joint-hands—*i.e.*, Bain's and Coney's—to manage for us.

Late in May there were many more evidences of spring. The nigger-grass had sprouted: I well remember May's delight with the first green blades I took her. A few days after, on bare patches amongst the snow, I found a few lovely flowers; we had no idea of their names, but spring had come, and we were charmed.

There was plenty of water now to wash with; there was plenty to wash the heaps of wash-dirt, and the results were good. I, being handy with tools, made them a cradle, or rocker, and some sluice-boxes.

There was much movement at the diggings: every one was busy on top, and the change from the drear monotony of the terrible winter was giving place to cheery looks and hopeful faces. One could tell that the arrival of running water had been made much use of in another way; for we hardly recognised some of our acquaintances, since they had been able to wash their faces successfully and put on clean clothing.

That May had the knowledge of what was in my mind respecting her, I believed; but she carefully avoided giving me the opportunity of telling her about it. Why, she cannot even now explain, but so it was.

Towards the end of May the sun had much power: no snow was lying in the open, but the land was in a terrible condition; the deep grass and moss, saturated with water, was a perfect morass, all but impossible to get through on foot. The trails between the shanties and to the diggings were mere ditches. Those who had not good rubber or waterproof boots, or, better still, *muclues* —which is the native name for mud moccasins, the soles of which are made waterproof with seal oil—were in a bad plight; for the water was icy cold, and we believed that there would soon be much sickness amongst these unfortunates. We noticed, however, that the miners were very good to each other. If one was known to be badly off for foot-gear, food, or clothing, those who were better supplied shared with and helped them.

So far as we could judge, they were all a very decent, friendly crowd of men. We heard of no quarrels or rows amongst them, and saw none of that roughness and dissipation with which such gatherings are generally credited.

It is true there was no whisky there at all; all hands were by force teetotallers. Tea, strong and often, was drunk in gallons by every one.

We were impatient. The days passed very slowly with me and May, for we were longing to be off; but every one assured us that, even if we were then at Dawson, we should not be at all advanced, as we must wait there till the middle of June at least. No boat would yet start to descend the Yukon. Many who were said to know all about it declared it was often July before one could get away with safety.

But on the 1st of June we determined to wait no longer; and, after much discussion, we stowed our gold and what furs and gear we wished to bring home in our boat, which we had recaulked and repaired, and, accompanied by Frank and Coney, we embarked.

It was with mingled feelings we did so. Undoubtedly we were glad enough to be really on our way to England. But to leave the Bains was not pleasant: we regarded them, and they still are, amongst our truest and best of friends. Besides them, there were several other good fellows to whom we had become attached. Naturally, all were down to the water's edge to see the last of us, and to give us good wishes for our journey; nearly every man of them from the old country gave us letters and messages for their friends at home. We had a big bundle of the former, which we were pledged to deliver personally.

We brought Patch with us. May would not hear of parting with the dear dog until it was absolutely necessary.

We started at daybreak. The current was swift, and the river was clear of ice; but along its margin much was still piled up, besides logs and rubbish. By noon the water had risen considerably, and was floating this stuff off, making it unsafe to travel; so on a sort of knoll or island in the stream we camped.

At night, in the mountains, and at the heads of streams, frost holds sway, then the flow of water is arrested. But when the sun's heat melts the snow and ice up there, the body of water is increased and the current accelerated.

We met several parties coming up the river—very hard work they had. The rush had begun already there. On the fourth day we reached the Yukon and Dawson City.

As we neared the main river we had still more evidence of the rush. A very different state of things existed to that when we came up, and we met large numbers pushing up the Klondyke. We passed numerous camps, and heard from some of them wonderful accounts of what was being done up the tributaries of that river.

The topic was gold, naturally; but we also heard much about "grub," which appeared to be with many quite as important a subject. There was a scarcity of it, all declared, and there would be until the St Michael's boats arrived.

Small heed was paid to us: a few remarks were made about May, wonder was expressed at her being up there; but all were so absorbed in their own affairs that they took little interest in us, which was precisely what we preferred.

Dawson was all alive too. The river front was still encumbered with ice, but we were assured that it was dissolving rapidly. In places men were building boats or repairing them, in others they were stowing outfits into them: there were no idlers.

We landed just below the last shanty, and camped. Then Coney and I marched into the town. I was anxious to discover the store where I had found that nice Englishwoman when I went there before to buy the canoe. I had planned to speak to her about obtaining decent quarters for May.

I soon found the place, and had little difficulty; for after I had told this lady a portion of my darling's history and a few of her adventures, she begged me to bring her in and let her see her, any way. This I did at once; and they had hardly met before I was informed that May was to stop there until the boat sailed, which, we had ascertained, would be a week from the day we arrived.

Reports from down river, from Cudahy, had been received in some way, and were favourable.

There was only one steamboat at Dawson preparing to go down; very few were going in her. The captain was anxious to make a rapid passage, as he knew there were crowds of people at St Michael's, ready to pay big prices to get up. This just suited us, and I quickly secured our berths.

The Government official at Dawson—some called him governor, some colonel, others inspector, or commissioner—we found to be an exceedingly affable and kindly gentleman. Although he appeared to be overwhelmed with work, he gave me and Frank and Coney an hour of his time, during which he put all the business connected with our claims in order, and advised us what to do about the gold we had with us. Thus in two days after we got to Dawson City everything was settled, and we only had to pass the time as best we could until our noble ship should begin her journey out.

We had brought a canoe down with us for my companions to return in, as it would have been impossible for them to get our heavy boat up against that powerful current. We sold her to a party who had just come in from Lake Teslin: they had been camped there all winter. We obtained 150 dollars for her!

May being comfortably placed at the store with a very kind and hospitable hostess, we three men did Dawson—that is, we visited various stores, and examined their stocks and prices. There were plenty of fancy things—queer ornaments, toys, and suchlike—which one wondered should have been brought up, whilst of real necessities there did not appear to be a very great supply. The prices were enormous: we made very few purchases. We looked in at some of the saloons, saw what was called "life," and, being disgusted with it, concluded that up on the mines was far better for comfort and for pocket.

On the third day Frank and Coney, having had quite enough of it, started up the Klondyke for home. They took Patch with them: we could not take him down with us, and to have brought him home to England would really have been cruel—he would soon have died here. It was grievous saying farewell to that true and trusty friend.

Our parting with all of them was quite affecting. With these three, dog and men, was severed all connection with the horrors we had both experienced on the Klondyke and the Stewart.

With tear-dimmed eyes dear May turned her face from the Yukon, rushed down to the sea, and murmured—

"Now a new life begins for you and me, Bertie, my friend; but oh! how impatient I am to be off to England and my mother! How slow everything moves—everything but that great river!"

"A new life indeed," I responded, "and, please God, a happy one." And I wondered if part of hers would be passed with me. I wondered, and I hoped, and longed to ask her what she thought about it.

Dawson City was at that time merely a couple of strings of rough shacks and shanties, interspersed with all manner of tents and temporary shelters. One row of buildings ran parallel with the Yukon, and was called Front Street; the other, some distance behind, had no name then. All this part was on a low alluvial flat, said to hold gold enough to pay for working. The so-called streets were mere lines of rubbish-heaps and bog-holes. It was bad enough then; later, in the great heat of summer, pestilence would be sure to come, all said, for there was no attempt at sanitary arrangements. There were several large stores. Some had substantial warehouses attached to them: here everything was supposed to be supplied. All were of wood, naturally; some had iron roofs, some canvas, and some were covered with turf.

Every other building was a saloon, a restaurant, or a hotel. These latter had the grandest, gaudiest names. There was the Métropole and Grand, the Queen's, the Victoria, the Rossin House, and the Windsor.

The others, especially the saloons, were very fancifully christened. There was the Nugget, Woodbine, Mascotte, the Holborn Restaurant, the Elephant and Castle, and Delmonico's!

All were of logs, or sods, or slabs; many were built of old meat-tins, covered with sacking or even tarred paper!

There were a few women about. Many of these places were "run" by women. The less said about many of them who were famous then the better.

Naturally everything for sale was fearfully expensive, and gold-dust was the only currency. Every one carried gold about in a little buckskin bag called a sack: you see it sounded big to speak of a "sack of gold." On making a purchase, one handed one's sack to the storekeeper; he weighed out the amount, on the basis, then, of $17 per ounce. It was considered "bad form"—rather mean—to watch him too closely. What were a few grains of gold in those flush, glorious times?

Fortunately, we did not need to make many purchases. Our clothing was rough enough, truly, and terribly dilapidated, but every one was in the same condition: to have dressed better would have made us remarkable, and we desired to avoid notice. We could replenish our wardrobes in Victoria.

The headquarters of the mounted police in Dawson were very complete and substantial log buildings. They were kept in such perfect order that they were

an amazing contrast to the rest of the town. The
good old British flag flew over them constantly,
too.

Having arranged with the captain of the steamer
that I could occupy my cabin on board after my
friends had left, I found myself in clover. I took
my meals ashore, as I had discovered a decent place
where a fairly good meal could be had—fair, that is,
for the Klondyke—for one dollar. It was usually a
plate of pork and beans, with a piece of pie made of
dried apples or peaches, washed down with a basin of
what was called coffee. Sometimes salmon was to be
had, and once I struck bear meat, and once stewed
cariboo venison.

I saw May every day. We rarely went out
together. There was really nothing she cared to see,
and as all the roads and trails about this frontier
town were simply impassable with mud, and slush,
and knee-deep water-holes, there was no pleasure in
a walk. Another reason was that women—ladies—
being so rare there, her appearance on the street was
the cause of some excitement: people would waylay
us simply, I knew, to gaze with admiration on her
sweet face. May disliked this so much, and of
course I did, therefore she hardly went outside her
quarters during the week we were in the town.

With the help of Frank and Coney I had carried
our gold on board the boat, and had stowed it
amongst our furs and blankets. By the advice of

the commissioner I had informed the captain about it—he knew him to be a trusty fellow. We had kept the actual amount of it secret, which he and many others were anxious enough to know. The result of this was, of course, that we were credited with possessing as many millions as we had thousands: that mattered little, for if we had had nothing, every one would have reported us to be a mass of coarse gold and nuggets.

Robberies of anything but food, and those very seldom, were never heard of. All seemed to have perfect confidence in the honesty of the crowd. We Britishers and Canadians believed that it was in consequence of the presence of the splendid body of mounted police. No doubt they had much to do with it, but the Canadians are a law-abiding people, and the bulk of the foreigners had evidently great respect and confidence in the British flag and British law. The diggers, however, would have risen to a man to repel and punish any one found pilfering or gold-stealing. A species of lynch law had prevailed in that region for years, and the effect on the whole had made for good.

It was on the twelfth day of June that the steam whistle howled at daybreak, and our boat's bell clanged ceaselessly for an hour—how they *do* love noise over there!—and I brought May and her bundles on board.

The entire population of Dawson City came to the

water's edge to see us off, and yell their good wishes to us.

Then as the red sun arose across the yellow river, the stern-wheel began to beat the turbid stream, the ropes were cast off, and we were away.

May and I were at last started for England and home!

CHAPTER XIV.

Our vessel was a curious affair. The hull was a long, square-ended barge. In this was the engine which worked the huge wheel astern. On the deck a large cargo could be carried; over that were cabins, ranged along both sides, with the dining-room between. A railed passage—a balcony—surrounded the vessel on this deck outside the sleeping-rooms, and above all was the hurricane deck, where the passengers mostly passed their time.

The cabins were remarkably clean and comfortable: a Chinaman looked after them. Our food was excellent—considering.

The boat being "light," we were expected to make a record passage down — twelve days, the captain said; but it all depended on the state of the ice in the lower river.

There were only a dozen passengers besides ourselves—some of them were returning "sick," others because they were "sorry" they had come. Four or five were reputed to have made their piles. These were very silent men : they spent their time smoking, expectorating, and playing poker.

There was an American and his wife—Californians —who were very genial and superior : they were excellent company. There were also a young Englishman and an elderly Scotsman. The Americans were bound to San Francisco to buy goods: they had wintered in Dawson, and were returning later with their stock, and were going into storekeeping in Dawson in an extensive way. The Englishman and the Scot had done very well on Bonanza Creek : they owned they had made enough to live in Britain as they pleased.

We did not stop at Fort Reliance; it is all but abandoned, and has been so for years. That is where the first whites settled in that region, and it is from this point that most of the places have been named,—Forty, Sixty, Twelve Mile Posts were supposed to be these distances from Reliance. The Yukon is here five hundred yards in width; there are but few islands, and the current is regular.

At Forty Mile Post our boat was tied up for a few hours. This place is a small repetition of Dawson, although, I believe, a much older settlement: it is on the south side of Forty Mile river, which here joins the Yukon. It has several restaurants, billiard-halls, and bakeries, a blacksmith, and an opera-house !

On the north side of the river lies Cudahy, a smaller collection of stores and shanties. It has no

T

opera-house, and would, in consequence, be unhappy but for Fort Constantine, which was established in 1895. It is a station of the mounted police, who have several fine log buildings, so well cared for that they lend an air of civilisation to the place.

From here to the boundary line between Canada and the United States—the 141st parallel of west longitude—there is nothing worth noticing. The Yukon there is about the same width as at Reliance, but soon after entering American territory—*i.e.*, Alaska—it widens considerably. It continues thus for about one hundred miles, the banks on either hand being high and steep, with fine mountains inland. This portion is known as the Upper Ramparts.

Circle City we touched at. It had been a village of importance before Dawson existed. The Klondyke rush had taken away most of the inhabitants. We found it all but deserted. Here we took in wood for fuel, and heard with pleasure that the ice had left the river for a long distance down.

After this there are 150 miles of very much wider river, but it is a network of channels amongst small islands. Huge piles of ice were still to be seen on many shallows.

At Fort Yukon, which lies north of the Arctic Circle, we found hard winter reigned; but the river was free of ice. It is 380 miles below Dawson. The stream is said to be seven miles wide here. The navigation is most perplexing, as the channel shifts continually.

On the fifth day we came to floating ice, which extended from shore to shore. We moved slowly after it. It was drifting down at the rate of five miles an hour. During the short nights we tied up to the bank. At daylight, no ice being visible, we went on full speed until we overtook it. This continued till we were ten days out; then we came to a solid mass of ice, which was *not* moving.

Our captain, a bit of a philosopher, reckoned he had foreseen this delay and made light of it, but it was annoying to us.

There were no dwellings, no signs of human or any other life here, nothing but the dismal pine-clad river banks, where, being so far north, it was still deep winter.

We were stuck here four days. We were not a very lively party. Cards kept a few employed, and there were a few books on board. There were also a number of newspapers of the previous September. These were full of interest to some of us.

On the fourth day, suddenly, with an awful roar and turmoil, the ice broke up and started. We soon had clear water and went ahead again. No further stoppages occurred, we pushed on, and eighteen days from Dawson we reached the delta of the Yukon.

Here, the land being low and flat, and indeed then completely overflowed, we appeared to be on the open sea. We had to go eighty miles north through this to reach Fort St Michael, where our voyage in the stern-wheeler ended.

The few miserable settlements, trading-posts, and Indian rancheries which we had passed, or stopped at for firing, were all so perfectly uninteresting and monotonous that it is useless to even name them. The few inhabitants were generally busy in some way about the salmon. That fish was the all-absorbing topic here, as gold had been farther up.

We met but one vessel going in. She had been fast in the ice all winter, since the previous September! She was slowly pounding up against the strong current with so much of her cargo that was unconsumed during their long detention. What she had left was principally household furniture and whisky!—which would not feed the hungry.

Near St Michael's the mosquitoes discovered us, for it had now become intensely hot. Those pests stuck to us persistently until we were well out to sea.

May and I during this tedious time had become very friendly with our American fellow-passengers, Mr and Mrs Parker. May was so constantly with that lady that I had few opportunities of even a word with her, which made me quite unhappy. I fancied, foolishly, that May's past affectionately friendly way with me had ended, that she had changed, and that now that we were with others, and my help not so necessary, she was gradually forsaking me.

We were always in company, that is true, but she was never alone. It was rare now for her to call me Bertie, and I observed a look on her sweet face when I called her May which caused me to think she did not like it.

Yes, I was very miserable. I was jealous of her close association with Mrs Parker, I was jealous of the kindly way in which she spoke to that lady's husband. I was very absurd, I know. I was poor company then for myself, or for any one.

May had really changed very little in appearance, although she seemed to me to grow in beauty daily. With more civilised appliances, a few improvements in her dress, she became, in my eyes, the picture of all a girl should be. I longed to tell her this. I was annoyed, impatient, irritated at the obstacles which prevented me.

May always had a sad expression. Could one wonder at it? She was, I knew, still grieving over her lost father, and was anxious, filled with apprehension about her mother when she had heard the sad story she must tell her. I longed to help, to sympathise with her, indeed to be all in all to her, as I fancied I had been during that awful time up country.

It was very foolish, very preposterous of me, I am aware. I should have realised that such companionship could never be again, unless she became my wife. Really I knew it, and that is why I was so unhappy, and, as I see now, so stupid, for I then feared that she never could be that.

This state of matters continued until towards the end of this portion of our journey. It had grown so unbearable that I had become somewhat reckless. I really felt that I must put an end to it in some way. It actually came into my mind that I had better, on arriving at St Michael's, put her safely on board a ship bound for Victoria and return to Dawson and our claims up the Klondyke.

I said so to May one afternoon in the presence of Mr and Mrs Parker. I spoke as if I had all but determined to do so. She turned pale, then red. She did not speak, but she looked at me so eagerly, so imploringly, so frightened, that I was puzzled.

I was so abominably stupid that I attributed her expression of alarm to her fear of losing my help and guardianship. That she should be grieved at the mere prospect of parting with me, never entered my thick head that afternoon.

I said that I believed I should be better employed in looking after our interests up the Yukon than in going home in ease and luxury. "I'm sure you'll do very well and comfortably without me now, Miss Bell," I declared.

At this nasty speech the dear girl looked at me so surprised, so very sorrowfully, that I half regretted what I had said. She kept silence for a little. "Have you forgotten your promise to your friend

Meade? and to my poor father?" she asked me.

I replied, with difficulty, I admit, I was so dreadfully down-hearted and distressed, "Oh! you will do all there is to be done for Meade, I'm sure, as well, nay, better than I can, and so that I know all will be carried out as he wished, that promise will be kept; and your father's desire will be carried out too if I see you off safely from this country—and that I will do, most certainly."

"Are you in earnest, Bertie?" She seemed to be amazed.

I assured her that was how I felt then,—that I thought it would be much better so.

May was silent again. Shortly she arose and walked slowly to her cabin. I fancied I observed a tear trickling down her cheek as she left us. "She is thinking about the past," I said to myself.

That same evening, later,—indeed it was getting towards midnight — the sun had long set, but its brilliance was still in the sky—it did not leave it the whole night through at that season,—I was on deck, as I supposed alone, the steamer was pressing onward to the ocean down the rapidly flowing river, here quite broad. The distant mountains in the west and north towered up, violet, from a bank of rose-tinted mist, soft as carded wool. Here and there ice-clad peaks were still gilded by the sun, which was far down behind them, whilst the moon was riding full behind me. I was in deep distress, broken-hearted, yet I have a clear remembrance of the scene on which I gazed that night.

As I leant upon the rail and pondered upon what I and May had said earlier in the day, what our adventures together had been in the past, and what I had been foolish enough, as I at that moment considered, to imagine might be possible in the future, I was down-hearted and exceeding sad. My heart went out to May, I dwelt long and fondly on thoughts of her, but I could see no ray of hope, and could think of no reason why she should ever regard me as more than a friend; whilst I was longing, yearning, beside myself with love of her. "Yes, oh! yes," I muttered to myself, "it is far better that I part with her,—far better, indeed, that I return to my work away back in the north."

There was much vibration in the vessel. These craft are at best very fragile, very shaky. The beating paddle-wheel astern made so much noise that perfect quiet could not be attained anywhere on board.

I was somewhere amidships, the stillest spot that I could find, yet I heard no footsteps, and had no idea that any one was near me. Lifting up my eyes to heaven, I ejaculated something—I don't know what—some exclamation of despondency at the prospect of the life that I was contemplating in the Upper Yukon; but I do remember that I ended with the words, "And no May there!"

As I uttered them a hand was laid softly on my arm. I turned round hastily, and there my darling stood, gazing at me steadily, with tear-filled eyes. "Bertie!" she exclaimed, "Bertie, what do you mean? What ails you? Are you unwell? Are you in some new grief? What do you mean by crying out 'and no May there'? Tell me, my friend, my very dear friend, what is amiss, what you mean?"

I was speechless for a little while. What could I say? I only stared at her distraught, I was overwhelmed with emotion, and I could not prevent my looks showing what I felt. "Oh! May, May!" I murmured at last, "do you not understand? Do you not comprehend the misery that I am suffering?"

She was silent. She leant on the rail beside me, fixing her gaze upon the crimson glow beyond the mountain range. She was perfectly still and speechless.

My agitation was very great—she and I were at last alone. I knew that the time had come when I must speak out. It was, I felt, now or never, yet my tongue refused to form a sentence; the thoughts that were whirling through my brain refused to be turned to words. For several minutes we two looked straight before us, seeing nothing, and were dumb.

But in course of time I was able to speak; it was slowly and in broken sentences. "May," I began, "my dear friend May—my dearest friend—you are going home—shortly we must part. I am broken-hearted about it. You were such sweet company to me up in that fearful north; we have been through such awful scenes together. To me, though, they were the happiest times that I have ever known, or ever expect to know. I would willingly go back there, and end my days there, if you could be with me; but that being impossible, I have really, and truly, and seriously thought of late that it would be better for me to go back there alone, for I believe I should be happier in the scenes where you and I have dwelt together, where the memory of your dear presence will for ever cling, than at home in England separated from you." Then I was silent again.

Shortly after this outburst May asked me why we must be separated; why, if her companionship was so necessary to my happiness, I could not have it easier and better in England than in Alaska?

What was I to reply to this? I muttered something, and she went on—"Have we not laid our plans and schemes for our future lives? Are we not going to carry them out? We are well off now as regards money. We believe we can do all we wish, thank God. What, then, is troubling you? Why this sadness, this unhappiness? Why do you speak of parting company and ending it all, and adding a greater—yes, I will admit it, a greater grief to me than any I have to bear, by talking thus of putting an end to the life together which we have contemplated with so much delight?"

"Why—why do I do this, May?" I cried excitedly. "Why? because I love you—love you. Do you understand why, now? Don't you know that you are all the world to me, and more? Don't you comprehend that the entire future is dark and dreadful to me, because I love you, yearn for you, and have no hope of winning your dear love in return? That is the reason, May. Now you know this secret of my heart."

Again my dearest was speechless for some time: I saw the tears dropping, dropping from her sweet eyes; fain would I have clasped her to my heart and dried them, but I dared not.

"Bertie," she said then, softly. "Yes; now I know your secret. But why? oh, why are you so sure that you cannot win my love?"

I glanced at her bewildered. She turned to me, and I saw in her dear eyes a look I cannot describe, but I understood it. I was overcome with the joy of it, enchanted at the knowledge that suddenly flashed through my intelligence. I did not, could not, stop to analyse, but I knew she loved me. I knew that all my fears were follies, and that all my greatest desires, my fondest hopes, were granted, and that May was mine!

What I said or did then I have no clear recollection; only this, that I seized my beloved's hands and drew her to me as she laid her head confidingly on my shoulder and whispered softly in my ear, "Dearest, don't you know I love you?"

We remained on deck together for a long while. For my part I was in the seventh heaven of delight and thankfulness. I could not find words to make my darling understand how great my joy was. I could but kiss her and draw her to my heart, whilst she murmured again and again to me the joyful words, "Bertie, my dearest, best of friends, I love you."

We parted only when the sun was about to rise above the north-eastern ranges. I went below, a gloriously happy man. I went to my berth rejoicing that never-to-be-forgotten morning on the Lower Yukon in Alaska.

To our fellow-passengers we believed that there could be no apparent change in us when we all met; but to me and to May how different all things seemed to be. When I glanced at her across the breakfast table, and saw the love-light in her eyes, I knew that she was, as I was, filled with gladness unspeakable.

We hardly had three words together that morning, she was with Mrs Parker all the time; the whole forenoon she kept away from me. I hung around, smoked my pipe persistently, hoping every moment that she would join me—my face, I'm sure, showing my discontent.

She came at last, saying, "Don't you understand, my love, that we cannot be exhibiting to all these people what we are to each other? We must not expose ourselves to their remarks. Be patient; my thoughts are always with you."

"But why need you be with Mrs Parker always?" I enquired. "Surely no one will be scandalised if you and I walk the deck together, or sit beside each other. We used to do so three days ago; why cannot we do so now?"

"True," answered my sweetheart with a loving smile; "but we were not so self-conscious then. We know now what we are to one another; let us be patient."

Of course I was so full of rapture, so intensely pleased, that every syllable my dear one said to me had my immediate acquiescence. "Oh, yes," said I, "I will be patient; but why should not people know? Why don't you tell Mrs Parker of our happiness? She is a good woman, I feel sure, and if she knew the state of matters she would advise and help us. Don't you wish that you could tell the Bains and Sandy, eh? How delighted they all would be."

May did not tell me then, but afterwards she did, that Mrs Bain—woman-like—had discovered my darling's secret and mine also, and had prophesied to her what would happen "some day."

Not long after this I perceived May and Mrs Parker side by side, talking together intently, with so absorbed an aspect that I guessed what was their subject easily.

After supper that evening Mrs Parker, catching me alone, congratulated me, declaring that she had made up her mind about us before the boat left Dawson; and felt honoured that May had, at last, confided in her. She assured me that in all her travels, and amongst all her acquaintances, she had never come across a sweeter girl than May Bell.

So, thereafter, May and I had many a sweet hour together, contrived by this kind Yankee friend, who, having plenty of wit and common-sense, arranged for us.

I fancy every person on board knew that we were lovers by the time we landed at St Michael's.

This place is an irregularly built village on an island of the same name. It consists of a few large warehouses—Russian buildings—a few log and frame houses and stores, and, when we were there, many shacks and temporary huts and camps.

It is perfectly treeless, but the grass-covered rolling downs were so like the prairies of Manitoba that May and I were impatient to go ashore and feel soft green sward beneath our feet again.

Several large sea-going ships and steamers were alongside the wharf or anchored in the roadstead, and there were numerous river-boats loading and preparing for their passage up to Dawson.

It was very evident, even before our boat touched land, that there was considerable excitement here. We were the first people down that season; this caused a crowd—all the inhabitants it seemed—to meet us, eager for our report. They swarmed on board before we were made fast, vehemently demanding information. "Was it true?" "Was gold being got as they had heard?" "Was there any left?" This was the burden of their interrogations.

There were wild-eyed fellows amongst them, who tackled every man of us almost savagely. There were women, too, just as anxious to hear what we could tell. Some of these latter got hold of May, and the captain was surrounded by a clamouring mob. They hardly gave him the chance to make his ship fast.

He referred them to the miners on board for information. He particularly indicated me — then I was attacked with a vengeance. Questions poured upon me.

The intelligence I gave sent most of the crowd half-cranky with delight. At once they were for dragging me ashore and treating me with all the grog and good things the place contained. They declared that nothing was too good for me, for what I had told them satisfied them that they were not too late, that all the gold was not yet extracted from the Klondyke!

As for May, I saw her being haled ashore by her female admirers, and she was looking quite alarmed. So soon as I could get my besiegers to listen I begged them to let me go to her. They did so, but they all accompanied me, and were then for both of us accepting unbounded hospitality.

It seemed that our captain had let out that we had a lot of gold on board. We could not, and did not, deny this, but when it came to questions about the amount we answered mysteriously. That was enough; they were certain that the captain had been right when he put our treasure down as worth several millions!

It was some time before we could break away from these enthusiasts. Go where we would they followed us, each wanting a private word or two. It was an exciting time truly.

There was one fine steamship leaving for Victoria that very evening. With difficulty I got on board, interviewed her commander, a first-rate English sailor, and secured our passages. The Parkers did the same.

This ship, a well-known Victoria trader, had brought up a full to overflowing complement of passengers. She was returning empty for another lot.

We heard that Victoria, Vancouver, and all the inland towns of Canada, all the American cities on Puget Sound, with San Francisco and all California, were half-mad about these wonderful finds reported on the Klondyke. The latest news from Eastern Canada and the States, from Britain, and indeed from all the world, was that vast crowds were coming.

We heard such stories, such wild, astounding

stories about the doings up where we had come from. Such exorbitant fortunes that had been made, such heaps of gold-dust, such nuggets, buckets full of them! flour-barrels full! kegs heaped up with them! We were told that in some of the creeks the precious metal was so plentiful that men had picked up piles in a few hours—that there was plenty for every one who could but reach the Klondyke!

It was in vain that we assured them that *we* knew nothing of such occurrences,—that we were sure it was mostly gross exaggeration. No one would listen to this; they said we were trying to deceive them, to hide the truth from them, for that it was well known we ourselves had so much gold with us that we were multi-millionaires already, and were hoping and scheming to make ourselves richer still. It was no use our arguing, our disclaiming—they *knew* far better than we did.

We hardly heard a word about how the swarms, bound in, were to be fed. They knew that every ship had reached the port with heavy cargoes of food, they knew that the stores and warehouses here were full, but scarcely any one appeared to have an idea of getting it up to where the gold existed. They had very much to learn.

With some scheming we managed to get our gold transferred to this other ship; then we sailed at midnight.

This was a *real* steamship, flying the British

U

ensign, manned and served in proper British style. We had excellent quarters, a capital table—my darling girl and I were in the lap of luxury.

I need not particularise much about this voyage. We had good weather, bright, clear, and not so cold, for our 750 miles passage across Behring Sea to Dutch Harbour on the island of Unalaska, the most important of the Aleutian chain. Its mountains were capped with eternal snow, but the greenness of the lower land was very charming. Many vessels were lying here, as it is a supply station for the sealing and whaling fleets.

Here we remained but a few hours. We then entered the Gulf of Alaska, where a strong gale and a heavy sea was our fortune, as we steered almost due east, for 2000 miles, to Victoria.

Arrived there, we found an excited crowd to meet us. Newspaper men interviewed us, and the accounts they printed of what we had said and done, and of the amount of bullion we had with us, astonished, thrilled the world—*and us!*

We only remained two days in Victoria, at my old quarters at Bella Rocca. During that time we had to give full particulars to the authorities about Meade's and Mr Bell's deaths. We delivered our gold to the Bank of British Columbia, feeling great relief when it was safe at last. We replenished our wardrobes, and became again decent-looking and civilised members of society.

May cabled to her mother from Victoria—she merely announced that she was safe and well and on her way home. She also wrote to a relative, begging her to break the awful news she had to tell to her mother, as we both thought this would be better than May arriving and suddenly telling her dreadful story.

During our voyage from St Michael's to Dutch Harbour, May and I had a quiet time, and we endeavoured to plan our future movements. My desire was that we should be married in Victoria. I believed it would save much trouble and misunderstanding. But she would not agree to this. She declared that only at her mother's home would she become my wife.

We went on board the Yosemite late one evening, and were in Vancouver early the following morning, and about noon the same day left by the C.P.R. for Montreal.

At Vancouver we parted with Mr and Mrs Parker, who were to take the boat bound south for San Francisco.

There were many tourists on our train, old-country folk and Americans. The conductors were genial and polite; the porters attentive and kindly; the meals were excellent in the dining-car; the beds were wonderfully comfortable. It was a truly enjoyable trip we had through the Selkirks and the Rockies. We gazed with sad interest at the scenery about Banff, then we bowled across the prairies past

Broadview, where the train, stopping for an hour or so, gave us the opportunity of greeting a few old friends.

After five days' travel we arrived at Montreal, stayed at St Lawrence Hall for two days, then went on board the Allan steamer Parmesian, and sailed for home.

It appeared that the good folk of Victoria must have told the people on the Yosemite about us, and they must have passed the story on to the officials of the C.P.R. at Vancouver, for every one seemed to know where May and I had been, and what our experiences were, also the amount of gold we had brought out with us. Every one was attracted to us: we were famous, and had to answer no end of questions, and repeat again and again the story of our adventures.

We heard, and read subsequently, much about ourselves that was true enough, much that we certainly did not recognise.

There was the same experience on board the Parmesian, old and young seemed to be proud to hold a few minutes' conversation with either of us; but my dear girl was undoubtedly the heroine.

May had become splendidly well. She was very cheerful, too. I did my best to keep her from dwelling upon sorrowful memories.

When we reached England she was, as I was, thankful indeed; but now that she would be so quickly with her mother, she became very low-spirited and anxious. She dreaded, yet longed for, the sad meeting. She feared the effect upon her of what she had to say.

I accompanied her south as far as Maidstone, where a cousin met her, and she left me to hasten to her mother's arms.

* * * * *

Since that day three months have elapsed. A week ago there was a wedding at Chart Sutton, where Mrs Bell has been residing since her husband and her daughter went to Canada.

On our wedding-day Mrs Bell had sufficiently recovered her health and peace of mind to be present at the ceremony. My two brothers were with me, and many of May's friends. Meade's mother and sister came, so did Fanny Hume.

We have bought a little place near the sea, at Bexhill, in Sussex; that is where our home is to be.

There is some talk of my going out to the Klondyke in 1898. I think it is my duty. My wife is dead against it. She has made me promise, at all events, to wait until reports can be received from Bain and Coney. They are due in June.

* * * * *

At the end of June 1898 a letter came to hand from Bain. It was written in March, and was brought out by the "Yukon Kid," a famous half-breed, on his dog-train, over the White Pass to Skagway.

Bain reported that soon after we left they sold their claim at a good price; then they all moved up to Meade's Creek and built a comfortable cabin. Sandy Bain went down as far as St Michael's, bought a good outfit of stores, and was luckily able to get them up to Dawson by an early boat.

May's partners returned. They came in over the Chilkoot Pass, also bringing a good supply of food. They were grieved to hear of what Mr Bell and his daughter had suffered, and of the sad events that had ensued. They declared that they had made what they felt satisfied were reliable arrangements for their relief and rescue as they passed through Dawson the previous autumn. They approved of the way in which May had left the claim, and recognised Bain's and Coney's right to receive her share of the gold they obtained, which they promised to hand over at the proper time. The claim was looking still most prosperous.

Meade's Creek was staked out for miles above "discovery"—that is, our claim, Meade's and mine —and for some distance below. So was the creek upon which May's party's claim was situated. Trails had been cut, and on each creek a store or two had been started. A log church had been erected on Meade's Creek. Service was held by volunteers almost every Sabbath.

About the gold, Bain had very good news to tell. The dump which we had left had been washed. It was very rich. They had hired men to work for us, who had already got out another heap that looked to be as full of gold as ever. They had knocked away most of the hill in which we had our dug-out and our tunnel.

Bain's own claim looked well. They had already secured such an amount of gold, that he and his wife had serious thoughts of coming home the following autumn, leaving Frank and Sandy to go on mining, or to sell out when they got an offer good enough. He finished the business part of his letter by suggesting that I should await further reports before starting for the North-West again—that is, if I had any thought of coming. There was also some information about the route in by Skagway, on which he said great work was being done. A road for vehicles was completed, bad places had been bridged, &c. A railroad was commenced over the White Pass, and by the spring of 1899 it was confidently expected that it would be completed to Lake Bennet, the head of the navigation. Steamboats had been constructed to traverse the lakes and rivers. Stores, bunk-houses, and shelters had been erected along the trails. A tramway had been constructed round Miles Cañon and White Horse Rapids, and vast quantities of stores had fortunately been brought up from St Michael's, so that no great fear of starvation existed.

An aerial wire-way, which he thought little of,

had been erected over the Chilkoot pass. It carried no passengers, only merchandise and stores.

Thus it appeared that as in this short time such immense improvements had been made in the way in to the Klondyke, we might expect in a year or two to be able to go in and out with speed and comfort in summer and autumn. But during the long and terrible winter there would be no easy way until a railroad was established.

There was an enclosure from Mrs Bain to May. She sent her loving messages, and hoped before her missive reached her she would be May Singleton. Which is exactly what she is.

Patch was flourishing—every one's favourite.

So I end our story. We are waiting for the latest news from Meade's Creek. But if no more gold is obtained from our claim on the Klondyke, we have reason to be well content, and to be thankful to the Giver of all good for His bounty to us.

THE END.

www.ingramcontent.com/pod-product-compliance
Lightning Source LLC
Chambersburg PA
CBHW021149230426
43667CB00006B/318